Cro-Magnon Man

TIME
LIFE
BOOKS

WORLD WAR II
THE SEAFARERS
THE TIME-LIFE BOOK OF BOATING
THE GOOD COOK
TECHNIQUES OF PHOTOGRAPHY
THE TIME-LIFE ENCYCLOPAEDIA
OF GARDENING
HUMAN BEHAVIOUR
THE GREAT CITIES
THE ART OF SEWING
THE OLD WEST
THE WORLD'S WILD PLACES
THE EMERGENCE OF MAN
LIFE LIBRARY OF PHOTOGRAPHY
TIME-LIFE LIBRARY OF ART
FOODS OF THE WORLD
GREAT AGES OF MAN
LIFE SCIENCE LIBRARY
LIFE NATURE LIBRARY
YOUNG READERS LIBRARY
LIFE WORLD LIBRARY

The Emergence of Man

Cro-Magnon Man

by Tom Prideaux
and the Editors
of TIME-LIFE BOOKS

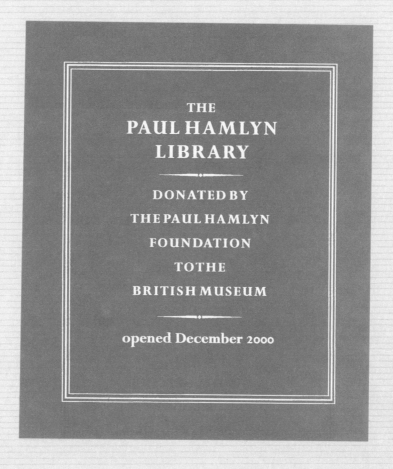
TIME-LIFE INTERNATIONAL

(Nederland) B.V.

The Author: For more than 25 years an editor and drama critic for LIFE, TOM PRIDEAUX is the author of two books in the TIME-LIFE Library of Art, *The World of Delacroix* and *The World of Whistler*. Mr. Prideaux is also the co-author, with Josephine Mayer, of *Never to Die*, a book on ancient Egypt, a subject that first roused his curiosity about the men who came before the Egyptians.

The Consultants: PHILIP E. L. SMITH is Professor of Anthropology at the University of Montreal, and an expert on late Palaeolithic cultures in Europe, North Africa and the Middle East. RICHARD KLEIN is Associate Professor of Anthropology at the University of Washington. His speciality is early man in southern Africa, but he is also known for his summaries of Russian archaeological material.

The Cover: Crouched on a ledge in a narrow passageway deep inside Lascaux Cave in southern France, a Cro-Magnon painter puts the finishing touches on the last of a series of little horses. The figure was painted by Burt Silverman on a photograph of the cave taken with artificial illumination —hence the somewhat brighter light than a prehistoric artist's flickering oil lamps would have provided.

Contents

Introduction

The period covered in this book—the ending of the last ice age, from roughly 10,000 to 40,000 years ago —was the supreme age of the hunters and gatherers, and the last one in which they dominated the human scene. Soon afterwards, new and different forms of adaptation would lead to agriculture and the rise of towns and cities.

The great age of the hunters and gatherers has fascinated many prehistorians for a century. Some may unconsciously have seen it as a kind of last stand of "natural man". Others have perhaps seen it as a necessary stage, a proving ground for ideas and techniques that were to lead man to a higher level of knowledge and self-awareness. Still others have wondered if the limits of man's self-expression had been reached with the magnificent cultures that flourished at the end of the last ice age in Western Europe and produced the brilliant cave paintings.

Undoubtedly part of the attraction of this period is that its cultures seem to have been made by men like ourselves—men who, in the 19th Century, came to be called Cro-Magnons. Rightly or wrongly, this expression has floated away from its original home in southwestern France and become attached to populations of prehistoric hunter-gatherers who never came near the cliffs at Les Eyzies where the first Cro-Magnon remains were found in 1868.

Cro-Magnon man is now regarded by many as the epitome everywhere of Homo sapiens sapiens. Archaeologists and physical anthropologists know that things were a great deal more complex and that the term (whether used to denote a physical type or a genetically related population) has probably been stretched to its limit, even in Europe. And yet however much they may deplore its usage in so broad a sense, students of the past recognize that they are fated to have to live with the myths and misconceptions that their professional ancestors promulgated all too successfully. The term Cro-Magnon man has become ambiguous and imperfect, but it promises to be with us for a while.

The use of Cro-Magnon in the title of this book, which deals with preagricultural modern man in all parts of the world, may thus offend a few purists, but the subject matter treated by the author is hard to overvalue. Scholars may not know precisely when the era of modern man began, or when exactly it ended, but they do know that by 40,000 years ago, in several parts of the Old World, a series of new cultural shifts and emphases appeared. While by no means divorced from what went before, events henceforth began to move in a different direction and at a different, speeded-up tempo—and the prime mover was now man himself.

Having inherited from more primitive ancestors large and efficient brains, as well as a serviceable technology, these new humans proceeded to make a quantum jump greater than anything seen before in a comparable length of time. In aesthetics, in communication and symbols, in technology and adaptive efficiency, and perhaps in newer forms of social organization and more complex ways of viewing their fellows, these first modern men went on to effect a transformation worldwide in its impact. Without their accomplishments the world—and we—would be very different today.

Philip E. L. Smith
Professor of Anthropology
University of Montreal

Chapter One: The Arrival of Modern Man

Hell's Gorge, it looked more like a little pastoral par-

Although the place was called Gorge d'Enfer, or
Hell's Gorge, it looked more like a little pastoral paradise. I entered it by a lane that turned off the main
road about a half mile outside the village of Les Eyzies in the Dordogne region of southwest France. The
lane sloped upwards through an open wood of ivy-
covered tree trunks. The ground was soft with moss,
but among the trees jutted several huge overhanging
rocks. They provided ready shelter that afternoon
against the spurts of spring rain, just as they doubtless did for the ancient men who inhabited this region
30,000 or 40,000 years ago—the terrain here has not
changed drastically since then. I suppose the place
got its modern name from the craggy rocks which,
perhaps viewed by moonlight, struck some melan-
choly Frenchman as infernal.

My visit to the gorge was by appointment to meet
Christian Archambeau, supervisor of prehistoric digs
in the Dordogne. Normally, the public may visit most
of these sites, caves where the remains of early man
have been found in great numbers, simply by going
to a near-by farmhouse and asking the farmer or some-
body in his family to serve as a guide. For a small
fee, the guide unlocks the metal barrier at the cave entrance, turns on the interior lights and guides you
through. But at one of the places I tried to see, Les
Combarelles, the guide was sick, and I had been told
how to locate Archambeau, who had keys to all local
caves and would give me a conducted tour.

*One of the earliest portraits of man, this Cro-Magnon profile
was carved on a hard limestone plaque some 13,000 years ago
and left in a cave near Vienne in the upper Rhone Valley.
Though the figure's nose and jaw are curiously elongated and
the cheeks oddly scratched, the skill of the artist is evident
in the well-shaped eye and the bold outlines of the neck.*

The only hitch, as I soon discovered, was that Archambeau had gone to the gorge to join a dozen other
men in the unlikely enterprise of uncrating a bison.
The bison was in a big box that looked like an upright-
piano case, roped onto the rear of a truck, and the animal had travelled more than 300 miles from the
Vincennes Zoo near Paris. Now the truck was backed
up to a large enclosure built of rough logs. In a flurry
of last-minute work, the men were pounding extra
nails to strengthen the wooden bars and were adding
extra logs to keep the tenant securely inside.

When I found Archambeau, he explained that the
bison was part of a plan to create in the Gorge d'Enfer a small menagerie of animals allied to those that
used to roam here in prehistoric times. He led me up
the lane to a fenced-in meadow to look at some mou-
flons, or wild sheep, and in another meadow I saw
two wild asses, *Equus hemionus*, animals related to
the horses and asses that thrived here in the warmer
intervals of the last ice age.

After two busy hours, the bison's home was just
about ready. Final preparations were being super-
vised by a black-bearded zoologist from the Vincennes Zoo. Two tubs of spring water and a pile of
hay garnished with carrots were put inside the enclosure. When the crate was finally tilted off the
truck, the bison pounded furiously with his hoofs at
the walls of his dark cell as he felt his world toppling
around him. Then, after the crate had been edged
into the enclosure entrance and a sliding panel was
lifted slowly from the bottom, a single black hoof
was thrust out. And then a hairy leg. It seemed as if
the bison were being born, pushing his way from the
womb. Suddenly he lurched free completely, took a
few wobbly steps and then looked around him, stupe-

fied. "*Ah, pauvre petit,*" said the bearded zoologist.

When he was satisfied that his charge was properly lodged, he told me that it belonged to an almost extinct breed called *Bison bonasus*, a close relative of the completely extinct *Bison priscus* that had been hunted, eaten and pictured by the prehistoric men of Europe. Herds of the heavy-maned *bonasus* had once inhabited these grassy plains; in later times they were exhibited in the arenas of Caesar's Rome. Now only a few hundred head of *bonasus* survive, most of them in a wooded official reserve in Poland, although they are apparently staging a gradual comeback in their protected situation.

Archambeau and I soon departed for Les Combarelles, where I renewed my admiring acquaintance with Stone Age art. But the bison stayed on my mind, and on my last morning in Les Eyzies, I returned to say goodbye to him. He was alone, munching some grass and scratching his head against a tree trunk. The hay and carrots were gone. I stuck my face between the logs of his stockade and he, mildly curious, came forward until his big shaggy head was close to mine. We both stared. The ridges and markings around his eyes made them look oddly mysterious, like the eyes painted on figurines found in ancient Egyptian tombs.

I cannot claim that we shared any mystic affinity, but I was touched by the nearness of him, a warm-blooded mammal like myself on the planet Earth, another marcher in the long parade of evolution. We were simply passing in transit, he on his way out, perhaps, and my species still on its way in, presumably. Yet I was curiously moved by the bison. He served as a living link to the far distant past, transporting me back towards the world of early man. When I was leaving the Gorge d'Enfer, I turned for a last look. The bison was standing immobile against the rock wall that formed the back of his enclosure, like a cave painting come to life.

It was fitting that we should have been there in the Gorge d'Enfer together—the bison a fugitive from prehistory, I a student of it—because it is situated in the middle of what has been probably the world's must fruitful prehistoric museum. It is a fair guess that in the last 100 years, more archaeologists have found more artifacts and remains of early men in the 3,500-odd square miles of the Dordogne district than in any other comparable patch of earth. And it was at Les Eyzies, about a mile from the gorge, that the first acceptable proof was found that modern men had actually lived in prehistoric times.

The discovery was made prosaically enough by a gang of road workers cutting into a hillside just outside the village. They dug out the earth from under an overhanging rock shelter located in one of the many limestone cliffs that loom over the village, and with the dirt came bones and what looked like stone tools. Scientists summoned to the site soon uncovered the remains of at least four human skeletons: a middle-aged man, one or two younger men, a young woman and a child two or three weeks old. They were buried with flint tools and weapons, sea shells pierced with holes, and animal teeth similarly perforated, probably to make ornaments. The name of the rock shelter was Cro-Magnon, in garbled recognition of a local hermit called Magnou who had lived there. And so, the name Cro-Magnon was affixed to the new-found humans.

There was nothing unusual, of course, about finding human skeletons in the ground. But two things gave this find its unique importance. First, the consensus of the geologists who subsequently examined the site was that the remains were antediluvian, though they could not be dated exactly, and had belonged to creatures living long before the beginning of history. Moreover, it quickly became clear that those creatures had been men who in the flesh must have looked much like modern men. These assertions, inexact though they were, made heady reading in an age that by and large was satisfied by the Biblical story of Creation and that had no real concept of man's true antiquity.

But the whole truth about the Cro-Magnon remains, discovered in the years since, has turned out to be even more startling: the people of Cro-Magnon lived in that rock shelter some 25,000 years ago, and yet they were not simply like modern men, they were modern men. There was nothing ape-like about them. They had neither the beetled brows nor the sloping foreheads that had set apart all their human predecessors—Homo erectus and early Homo sapiens, including Neanderthal. The fact is that in scientific terms they were Homo sapiens sapiens, just as every human being on earth is today.

The people of Cro-Magnon were modern in every respect. Their physical differences from people living in Europe today were no greater than the differences now between Irishmen, say, and Austrians. On the whole, those ancient men were perhaps a little shorter than is the average European of today, their heads were a trifle larger—and also, perhaps, their brains. The men stood about 5 feet 8 inches on the average, had high foreheads, prominent chins, aquiline noses and small, even teeth. They were decidedly taller than the women, a characteristic that is also true of

Europeans today. Most scientists agree that since they resemble modern Europeans so much in their skeletal design, the people of the Cro-Magnon valley must have looked pretty much the same in other ways —their skin was probably light and of about the same hairiness as modern Caucasians.

There is every reason to believe that, given a proper education, Cro-Magnons in the world today would be able to master the intricacies of modern living. Their intelligence would be equal to the task—their problem would be one of acculturation. For the first modern men were hunters and gatherers, as all men had been before them, and their tools and weapons were still those of the Stone Age.

The Cro-Magnons would not depart from this nearly two-million-year-old way of life for many millennia to come. But they were equipped to initiate great changes, for they differed from their predecessors in more than physical appearance. They had greater intelligence. And they were the first humans to possess the mental and physical capacity to talk like modern men. The ability to exploit language fully was an asset of incalculable value, paving the way for revolutionary advances in human society.

These are the people whose remains were first found at Cro-Magnon. In the strict archaeological application, the name Cro-Magnon applies only to those who lived in southwestern France from about 10,000 to 35,000 years ago—a period in Europe technically known as the Upper Palaeolithic. But in a broader sense, the name Cro-Magnon is often used to refer to the first modern men everywhere. They appeared at different places on the earth at different times—the earliest date ascribed to their emergence is about 40,000 years ago—and their looks and behaviour varied locally, just as the appearance and customs of Japanese and Frenchmen differ today. But they all used stone tools of one kind or another and they all lived as hunter-gatherers—the last humans to live that way on a worldwide scale before man settled down into the Agricultural Age. Despite their physical and cultural differences, they can all, in a general sense, be given the label Cro-Magnon, and it will be used that way as a convenience in this book.

What the people of Cro-Magnon times accomplished is remarkable. They spread into all habitable regions of the globe, making their homes in every kind of environment any man since has managed to live in. They were the first humans to move into the arctic regions, learning to clothe and house themselves successfully against that inhospitable climate, and they were the first to set foot in North and South America, as well as on the continent of Australia.

Although their ancestors had been hunters for millions of years before them, these first modern men were the finest hunters of all, using new types of weapons and techniques to bring down prey of every kind and to exploit new resources, such as birds and fish, to a degree that had never been achieved before. At about the same time, many of them developed the practice of plant-gathering to a point that was just one step away from farming.

With the Cro-Magnons, technological man can be said to have come into existence. These people invented the first crude forms of baked pottery, constructing kilns and even burning coal. They presumably were the first to weave baskets as well. They made great strides not only in the preparation and use of stone tools but also in the elaborate development of tools, weapons and implements manufac-

Faces for Fossils

Is it possible to make an accurate posthumous portrait of a prehistoric man from a fossil skull? Many attempts have been questionable—different experts come up with different results even though they started with the same fossil. But Mikhail Gerasimov (*above*), a Russian archaeologist and artist, believed that the Cro-Magnon he re-created (*far right*) was true to life.

Gerasimov's confidence was based, in part, on his success in reconstructing faces from modern bones to help Russian police identify skeletons as missing persons. He deduced flesh contours from the sizes and shapes of the bones. Because his Cro-Magnon subject had wide-set cheekbones and large jaws that could accommodate protruding teeth arranged in a broad arch, Gerasimov determined that the cheeks were muscular and the lips fleshy.

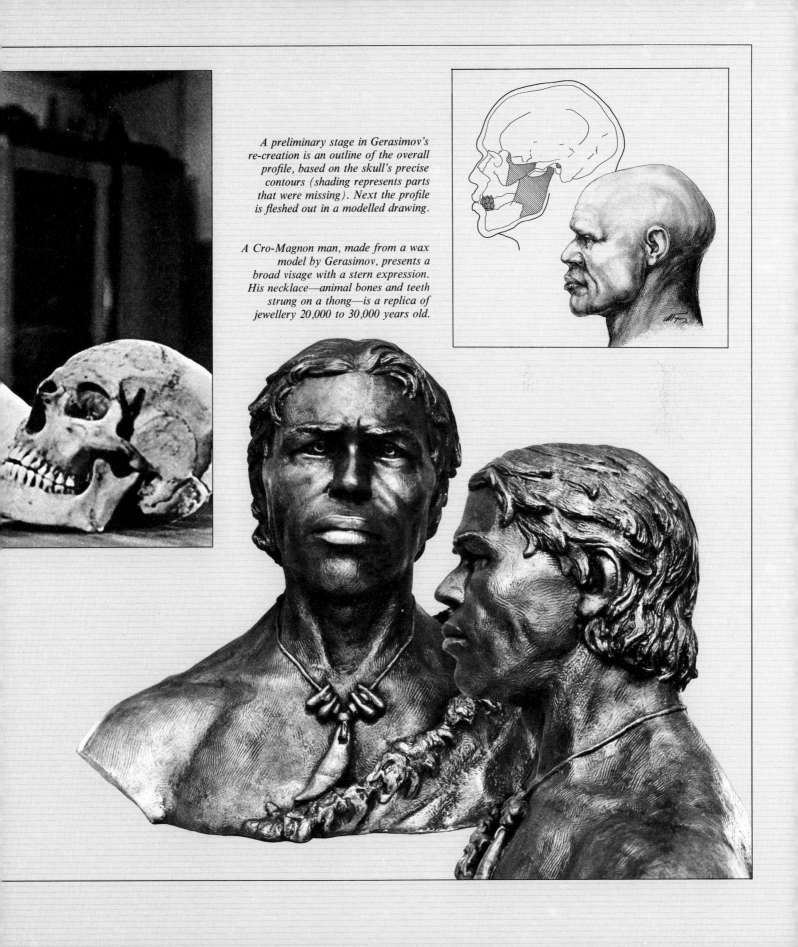

A preliminary stage in Gerasimov's re-creation is an outline of the overall profile, based on the skull's precise contours (shading represents parts that were missing). Next the profile is fleshed out in a modelled drawing.

A Cro-Magnon man, made from a wax model by Gerasimov, presents a broad visage with a stern expression. His necklace—animal bones and teeth strung on a thong—is a replica of jewellery 20,000 to 30,000 years old.

tured from bone, ivory and antler and, undoubtedly, wood. They fashioned better clothing, built hotter fires, constructed bigger dwellings, ate more kinds of food than earlier men had.

Perhaps most important of all the Cro-Magnon achievements was art. On the walls and ceilings of caves, in clay figurines, in decorated artifacts, these people exhibited an unprecedented artistic mastery. Never before had men expressed themselves with the aesthetic awareness that the Cro-Magnon artists displayed in even their humblest efforts. The best of their paintings and sculptures still rank among the world's greatest.

As these first modern men stretched their powers, they came to dominate nature in ways their ancestors could not have dreamed of. Their ability to exploit a variety of environments led to a great growth in their numbers, and populations increased as much as 10 times in some parts of the world. By the end of their time, some 10,000 years ago, they had set the stage for the last steps in the emergence of man: agriculture, the domestication of animals, metalworking, religion, writing, complex forms of social and political life, perhaps even for war.

In recent years prehistorians have begun to seek the origins of man in diverse parts of the globe—Africa, the Orient, Australia and the Americas. But the story of the first modern men properly begins in France, where four generations of archaeologists from many countries have excavated and analysed and argued since the first site was laid bare by the road builders of Les Eyzies in 1868.

In that quiet town it is hard not to feel the importance of the past, and its undeniable allure. After an hour or two of driving around the area, my strongest impression was that its very geology had been designed for human habitation, a huge open city, so to speak, whose architects had planned its broad crisscrossing valleys to run like wide boulevards between the limestone cliffs. The cliffs seemed peculiarly adapted for human abodes.

These masses of rock were formed more than a hundred million years ago by the accumulation of tiny lime-containing animals on the floor of the shallow ocean that once covered most of Europe. Untold billions of such creatures, little cement mixers, helped produce a building material useful to the future race of man. Strong and flexible, it was honeycombed and tunnelled by rivers and cascades, scooped into shelters and caves, levelled off into ledges, porches and overhangs.

The portal to one prehistoric cave, Font-de-Gaume, is halfway up a cliff that juts out into a little valley. On one visit to this cave, I paused just before going in and looked down on the valley below where a newly ploughed field stretched long furrows in the rich, brown earth. To a Cro-Magnon this cultivated field of the 20th Century would have been an inexplicable sight—the Agricultural Age invading the hunters' Old Stone Age—but in its overall aspect the view has probably changed little.

Suspended there between earth and sky, between past and present, I indulged myself in speculation about these earlier men, wondering what they had felt as they stood in precisely the same spot. I was particularly struck by the lordly authority and power that any human being might feel, gazing across a valley that so effectively commanded the approach of animals, friends or enemies.

Surely, over tens of thousands of years these cliffs had a positive effect on the formation of human character in this region. In a sense, they provided a stage setting that enabled man to elevate himself, to dramatize his position as sentinel and protector of his tribe. During the times when he lived here more or less permanently, the cliffs must have enhanced his sense of identity and contributed to early stirrings of community pride. Here were his burial pits, and also the secret shrines where rituals of the hunt were performed. Here were the scenes of his mating and the birthplaces of his children. Wherever he dwelled, to be sure, Cro-Magnon man doubtless began to develop a sentiment for home ground, a sense of belonging to a certain group or place. But the special beauty of the area around Les Eyzies must have aroused particularly strong attachments to home and hearth, and hunters returning after long trips in pursuit of big game could hardly have failed to welcome the sight of these lush valleys and protective cliffs with pride and satisfaction.

The Cro-Magnons were not the first human beings to occupy this beautiful place. Many of its caves and shelters had once been used by Neanderthals and even older men, whose tools and fossils have been found buried in the lower strata of cave floors. At Combe Grenal, for example, a cave about 14 miles from Les Eyzies, many thousands of tools probably made by Neanderthal men have been unearthed. Had Cro-Magnon men any awareness, conveyed by ritual or special art objects, of these former tenants of their home ground? It is impossible to say. But it is not far-fetched to think that they did associate with these places a dim sense of ancient presence that gave their homes an additional and powerful appeal.

A more concrete advantage of the Dordogne region was the extraordinary natural riches it offered its prehistoric inhabitants. The Massif Central, a mountainous plateau that covers most of central France, begins about 50 miles east of Les Eyzies. Its high plains would have been a fruitful summertime hunting ground that provided reindeer, horses and bison in abundance. West of Les Eyzies, the coastal plain stretching towards the Atlantic was also good grazing ground. The river Vézère ran then in much the same course as it does now, providing water and, to the later Cro-Magnons who learned to take advantage of it, a ready supply of fish. Many of the caves and shelters face south, offering maximum warmth and protection from the cold winds of winter. With all these amenities, it seems likely that, although many peoples of this time around the world were nomadic, following game through seasonal migrations, the hunters who dwelled in this fortunate region were able to stay in residence for the greater part of the year.

So it is not surprising that since man first came upon the rocks and valleys around Les Eyzies, about half a million years ago, the area has been as continuously and busily occupied as any other spot on earth. Men have clung like bats and barnacles to its cliffs and crannies, scattering their fossils and artifacts, leaving traces of their lives on walls and ceilings and buried underground. The human traffic through these crag-bordered ravines has been unceasing. Roman legions built walls here. Medieval noblemen erected castles and towers on rocky ledges, and turned the caves into arsenals, storerooms, hideouts and wine cellars. English soldiers occupied the caves in the 15th Century during the Hundred

Years' War, and bandits have hidden out in them for centuries. Today in Les Eyzies many little homes and buildings, including the village's best-known hotel, are snuggled up against these overhanging cliffs, which provide them with a fourth wall.

Considering the long duration and density of human occupation of this region, it seems fitting that the first accepted evidence of the first modern men should have been found there. At the time of the discovery in 1868, however, people were concerned less about where this apparently modern ancestor turned up than by the fact that he turned up at all. It was a time of heated debate over man's origins. Many people were furiously hostile to the suggestion, broached by a few scientists, that the human race was a very ancient one. Some intelligent Christians firmly believed the calculations made in 1650 by Ireland's Anglican Archbishop James Ussher, who said God created Adam in 4004 B.C. (Another ingenious cleric had even set the exact time: October 23 at 9 a.m.) On the other side of the question, though, the arguments for human antiquity were becoming harder to ignore.

In 1859 Charles Darwin had published *On the Origin of Species* which, in propounding the theory of evolution, suggested that life on earth went back beyond anyone's previous imagining. Darwin did not actually apply his theory to human development until more than a decade later, but the implication was there for those who would take it. Even more convincing was the accumulating evidence of fossil bones. In many places the remains of long-extinct animals were dug up, and mixed with them were human fossils—apparently the animals and the men had lived at the same time. If the animals were very an-

cient, the men must have been, too. Then in 1856 in the Neander Valley in Germany, a skeleton was found in very ancient rock layers. It seemed human, but its skull had many ape-like features, which the experts grossly exaggerated.

The Neanderthal man was not a creature anybody of the time wanted as an ancestor. He was an embarrassment, and the discovery of Cro-Magnon man, soon thereafter, came as an enormous relief. Cro-Magnon was certified prehistoric, and yet he was modern-looking—a perfectly acceptable member of the human family tree to those who were willing to accept man's antiquity but were not able to stomach evolution or acknowledge Neanderthal's kinship. If mankind was as old as the Cro-Magnon remains seemed to indicate, the argument went with undaunted logic, it was unlikely that man could have been involved in Darwin's undignified and heretical evolutionary process. Man must therefore always have looked the same. Cro-Magnon man, by contrast to Neanderthal man, was, in the words of one modern anthropologist, "the Apollo of prehistoric men". People of the 19th Century could identify with him, and he could plausibly support their Rousseau-bred fantasies about the noble savage.

To have achieved acceptance of the idea of prehistoric man on even these questionable grounds was a major breakthrough for the science of archaeology, and the advent of Cro-Magnon was a critical turning point for a discipline that was only just starting to clarify the mysteries of the distant past. Up to the mid-19th Century, man's interest in times gone by had centred mainly on the beautiful, the sacred, the valuable and the peculiar. Before the word "archaeology" came into common use—in the early 19th Cen-

The Cycle of Cave Men's Caves

The cave dwellings of early men were started by water seeping down fractures in limestone from a conifer-dotted plateau. The water, acidified by chemicals in the ground, gradually dissolved a hollow that enlarged, and eventually ate through the rock to the river, forming the cave's mouth.

In the Cro-Magnon period, after geologic changes had lowered the river level and drained the cave, the dry shelter was occupied by man. But the continued dissolving action of water weakened the cave roof and caused sections to collapse, creating sinkholes on the plateau. The water also hollowed out smaller caves underneath the floor of the larger one.

In modern times, the collapse of water-weakened limestone has blocked the cave's mouth and the sinkholes on the plateau are filled in with soil, dead leaves and broken limbs from deciduous trees that have replaced the conifers of earlier times. The original cave is closed—and its artifacts and bones sealed away.

tury—the favoured word was "antiquarianism". In the Middle Ages, few people had the wealth or inclination to indulge in antiquarianism. But with the great renaissance of arts and learning in 15th Century Europe, the collectors and connoisseurs began to multiply. Popes, cardinals, rich merchants and adventurous explorers competed fiercely to acquire treasures of the past.

As far back as the 17th Century, England's James I became a patron of archaeology when he ordered his brilliant architect, Inigo Jones, to investigate the mysterious Stonehenge on Salisbury Plain. Jones drew the first official plan of this ancient monument (begun about 2600 B.C.), and confidently pronounced it a Roman temple. This understandable mistake (after all, the Romans had built a wall across England) indicts Jones less than it does the prevailing ignorance of his day on all prehistoric matters. But, ignorant or not, commoners as well as kings began to concentrate on monuments and relics. John Tradescant, a gardener to Queen Henrietta Maria, set up his own eclectic hodgepodge of ancient oddities and called it a "Closet of Curiosities"; it formed the nucleus of Oxford University's great Ashmolean Museum.

By the 18th Century the human pack rats were on the march. Over the next 100 years, Byzantine fountains and Greek pottery, Egyptian obelisks and pediments from the Parthenon were toted across the sea and deposited in the great museums and public parks of Europe. A good deal of greed and arrogance accompanied these transactions, but there is no denying that the lordly antiquarians helped popularize the ancient past, promoted the habit of looking backwards and paved the way for their more serious-minded successors.

In the midst of this flamboyant piracy, evidence kept turning up of a past more distant than the antiquarians had been thinking of, a time stretching back before the classical ages recorded in history and myth. At the end of the 17th Century, a flint hand axe, obviously man-made, was found near the bones of an extinct elephant in London. This association, demonstrating the existence of men at some heretically ancient date, was embarrassing, and the evidence was denied. The elephant, authorities decided firmly, was a Johnny-come-lately that had been marched to England during the invasion of the Roman Emperor Claudius. The fact that Claudius had never, so far as could be determined, imported elephants to England did not seem to bother anybody.

A similar incident occurred in Germany in 1771, when a German pastor, Johann F. Esper, found some human bones in a cave near Bamberg in the same layers of soil that contained the bones of cave bears and other extinct animals. That they might have existed together certainly occurred to Esper, as we know by his own account of the finds. Regarding the human bones, he asked, "Did they belong to a Druid or to an Antediluvian or to a Mortal Man of more recent times?" Then he answered lamely, "They must have got there by chance." Still, the fact that Esper had framed the question at all was a milestone.

It is often assumed that organized religion hampered the progress of archaeology. To a degree, it did. But at the same time, several early archaeologists emerged from the clergy. In addition to Esper, a Protestant, there was an English Roman Catholic, John MacEnery, who carried on excavations for four years during the 1820s in Kent's Cavern near the English seacoast town of Torquay. Under the unbroken floor of the cave, Father MacEnery found many stone tools and weapons in conjunction with the bones of rhinoceroses and the remains of other animals long extinct in that part of the world. To him this was proof that these men and beasts had lived during the same period. But other churchmen did not agree. To William Buckland, a man of God who became Anglican Dean of Westminster and was also a noted geologist, the young priest was wrong. How did the tools get embedded in these ancient rock strata? Well —the dean must have thought fast—the "Ancient Britons" had dug deep holes to be used as ovens in the cave floor. And somehow they had carelessly dropped, or hidden, their tools in these holes, which conveyed them into the lower strata with the rhinoceros bones. No matter that there was no trace whatsoever of ovens in the cave floor. Buckland was highly respected as a palaeontologist and geologist as well as a cleric, and MacEnery bowed to the man's powerful reputation.

Before long, the new science of geology would come to the rescue of the embattled prehistorians who were trying to prove man's antiquity, providing objective measures for the age of earth formations in which human bones were being found. But for a time the geologists were more hindrance than help. They spread a popular theory, called Catastrophism and endorsed widely by Dean Buckland and the French naturalist Georges Cuvier, according to which the earth had once suffered a sudden Noachian deluge —or a series of deluges. In these catastrophes men, animals and human artifacts were tossed and tumbled in chaotic disorder. Catastrophism seemed to explain how old and new bones were jumbled together, and why marine specimens were often found on mountain tops and in deserts. This explanation knocked the pins out from under any archaeological theory that held human fossils to be contemporaneous with whatever other animal fossils shared their burial grounds.

Catastrophism was short-lived. It was killed and supplanted by Uniformitarianism, a concept whose chief spokesman, Sir Charles Lyell, had once been a pupil of Dean Buckland. Lyell published in 1830 a work called *Principles of Geology*, which denied that the earth had suffered sudden and violent cataclysms. Instead, he maintained, the planet is perpetually undergoing changes at a uniform rate—hence Uniformitarianism. Most of the upheavals that went on in bygone ages are still going on today, Lyell hypothesized. Mountains are always heaving upwards or crumbling away. Winds unceasingly hone rocks. Ice and water are constantly at work, reshaping shorelines and rearranging deserts and jungles. Volcanic lava is continuously simmering or boiling over, and the earth's old crust is always cracking and twitching. The only reason this process is not noticeable is that it occurs so slowly, in terms of a human life span, that it can seldom be seen happening. In Lyell's later years, he modified his theory a little, granting that the rate of change may quicken or slacken somewhat from age to age. But in essence his theory has proved to be true, and is now generally accepted.

Uniformitarianism was the key to the rational study of man's origins. By affirming that successive layers of rock are piled on the earth, usually in chronological order, this concept buttressed the belief that objects embedded in a particular layer are *ipso facto* contemporaneous with that layer. Today this assumption sounds so completely reasonable that it

Text continued on page 24

A Cosy Home in the Rocks

A traveller following the tortuous course of the river Vézère in the Dordogne region of France (*map at right*) can easily see why this valley became an ice-age population centre. The rock here is limestone and, thanks to its yielding character, the steep cliffs that flank the valley have been pitted and honeycombed by water and frost, forming hundreds of protected sites suitable for human habitation.

The deep caves and shallow rock shelters did more than serve as refuges for Cro-Magnon hunters. In some places the weakened limestone collapsed, sealing off a rich heritage of Cro-Magnon art and artifacts that only in recent times has come to light.

Seen from a cliffside ledge north of Les Eyzies, the Vézère Valley presents a peaceful panorama little changed since Cro-Magnons surveyed the scene. At left, the ledge leads past a shallow rock shelter, one of hundreds of prehistoric dwellings that are still unexcavated.

On top of a 150-foot-high cliff rising almost vertically from the water, two rock shelters are visible as dark holes. They were warmed by winter sun, for this section of cliff faces south in a jagged wall below the town of Limeuil, where the rivers Vézère and Dordogne converge on their way to the sea.

The Vézère, shown here with its important Cro-Magnon sites, twists 119 miles across a limestone plateau in southwestern France (inset map) before it joins the Dordogne, for which the surrounding region is named. The Vézère is lined with bigger, more numerous rock shelters and caves than the Dordogne, and became a population centre for Cro-Magnon man.

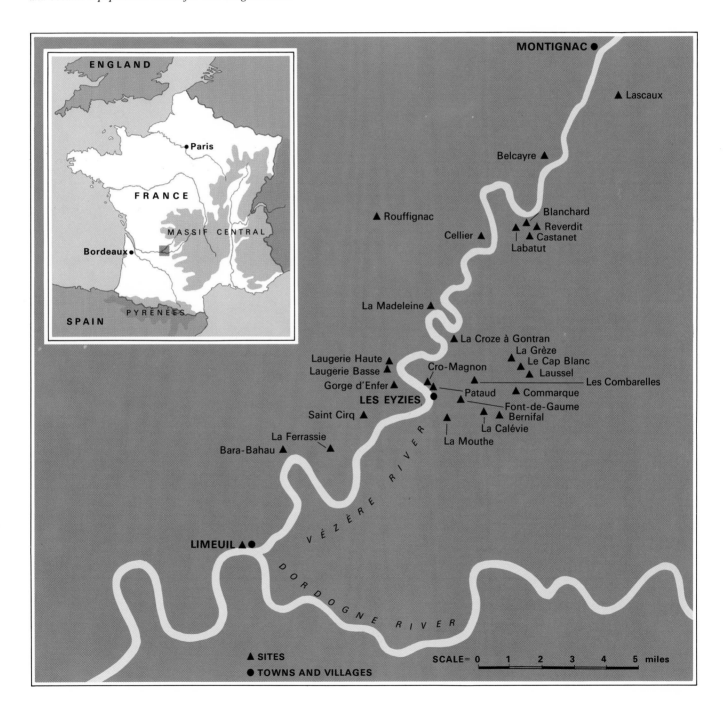

Protected by jutting walls and a 100-foot overhang, the broad floor outside a limestone cave in the Gorge d'Enfer made an ideal living space for ancient families. The 12-foot-high cave entrance, at centre, leads to a small chamber. Many deep caves, hollowed out by circulating water, were used for wall paintings, burials and possibly ritual ceremonies.

A rock shelter overlooking the river Vézère resembles the protected cave mouth at left, but is the smaller product of a different and swifter process. Beneath the overhanging ledge of hard limestone are softer layers that were slowly broken off by repeated freezing and thawing. In time this ledge, like many others, will be undercut until it collapses.

is hard to believe it was once a world-shaking idea.

While the Englishman Lyell was establishing a logical method for dating archaeological finds, Danish scientists were working out a practical way of classifying prehistoric artifacts: the Three-Age system, which divided the past into Stone, Bronze and Iron Ages. The Danes, who had been cut off from the main flow of the European Renaissance, took an intense pride in their own early culture; by law, all citizens had to submit to the royal collections any ancient-looking objects they found in the ground. The Danish archaeologists deplored the fuzzy thinking of many Europeans, who could not conceive of ancient times as an orderly succession of periods but lumped everything together in a vague, romantic stockpile of Roman ruins, Celtic fossils and Druidic leftovers. So an antiquarian named Christian Thomsen organized the collected pieces according to the material they were made of. He and his co-workers were a powerful influence for order and system in prehistoric studies, and the Danes have been called, with justice, the real founders of archaeology.

The new science seemed to produce a new breed of men, independent, dedicated and obstinate—often to the point of eccentricity. A leader in this colourful company was Jacques Boucher de Crèvecoeur de Perthes. Born into a prosperous French family, he was a man of considerable versatility: a soldier for Napoleon, a novelist, a man-about-town, a candidate for parliament (never elected), a writer of plays (never performed), a champion of women's rights (never married). But most important for the story of mankind, Boucher de Perthes served for a time as a customs official at Abbeville, a northern French port.

There he had the prehistoric past almost dumped right in his lap when dredges working along the river Somme began scooping up man-made tools, among them a polished axe hafted in stag horns.

Boucher de Perthes' excitement was immense. Further search turned up many more implements buried along with the bones of extinct animals, and he made the logical deduction about their extreme age. Boucher de Perthes published eight volumes on his finds and convinced some of his countrymen of man's prehistoric existence. But his discoveries were noted with derision at the fountainhead of France's scientific life, the Academy of Sciences of Paris.

The Frenchman's zeal might have come to nothing had not the news of his labours reached England. In 1859 two English scientists, Joseph Prestwich and John Evans, visited Boucher de Perthes and inspected his digs at Abbeville. They were especially impressed because the excavations confirmed what a few of their own compatriots had also claimed about the antiquity of man on the basis of fossil discoveries in Brixham Cave and Kent's Cavern in Devon. The tide was turning. Boucher de Perthes was lauded and honoured by English scientists in papers read to the Royal Society in London.

Edouard Lartet, a respected jurist and palaeontologist in Castelnau-Barbarens, a village in southwestern France, had for years been excavating in the Pyrénées foothills. At first Lartet had been able to afford only an amateur's interest. But after publishing several important papers on the subject, Lartet captured the attention of a rich London banker and amateur ethnologist, Henry Christy, who not only offered to subsidize Lartet's researches but came to France to work with him. The French-English team,

The Pains and Perils of Early Archaeology

The dangerous working conditions, the inadequate funds and public ridicule that hampered the pioneers of archaeology are illustrated in the career of a Belgian doctor, P. C. Schmerling, who in 1830 uncovered two human skulls mixed with mammoth and rhinoceros bones—proof of their ancient age. He had to wait a quarter of a century to receive the recognition his discoveries deserved. Then the English geologist Sir Charles Lyell paid sympathetic tribute to Schmerling in The Geological Evidences of the Antiquity of Man—summing up his trials and achievement in a rousing marathon sentence:

To be let down day after day, as Schmerling was, by a rope tied to a tree so as to slide to the foot of the first opening of the Engis cave, where the best preserved human skulls were found; and, after thus gaining access to the first subterranean gallery, to creep on all fours through a contracted passage leading to larger chambers, there to superintend by torchlight, week after week and year after year, the workmen who were breaking through the stalagmite crust as hard as marble, in order to remove piece by piece the underlying bone breccia nearly as hard; to stand for hours with one's feet in the mud and with water dripping from the roof on one's head, in order to mark the position and guard against the loss of each single bone of a skeleton, and at length, after finding leisure, strength and courage for all these operations, to look forward, as the fruits of one's labour, to the publication of unwelcome intelligence, opposed to the prepossessions of the scientific as well as the unscientific public—when these circumstances are taken into account, we need scarcely wonder, not only that a passing traveller failed to stop and scrutinize the evidence, but that a quarter of a century should have elapsed before even the neighbouring professors of the University of Liége came forth to vindicate the truthfulness of their indefatigable and clearsighted countryman.

from 1863 onwards, began a series of major excavations in the Les Eyzies area, with its limestone cliffs, that would eventually make the Vézère Valley as crucial to the study of prehistoric man as the Valley of the Kings is to the history of ancient Egypt.

By 1867, the march of archaeology reached a milestone in the grand Exposition Universelle in Paris. Sponsored by Napoleon III, the big fair paid homage to industry and culture. It introduced an oddly ominous vehicle called a *batteuse*, or locomobile, that was supposed to prove useful as a steam-driven thresher. The United States, though still shaken by the Civil War, sent a display of rubber goods, including a life raft, and a new drink—much sampled in the American bar on a gaslit promenade—called a mint julep. As a bow to ancient culture, a replica was built of Egypt's Temple of Philae on the Nile. But far more ancient, and more astonishing, was a small but comprehensive exhibit of prehistoric artifacts, assembled from all over Europe.

The visitors peered at elegantly shaped flint lance heads from Dordogne and hand axes found in the Somme Valley. The real crowd-catcher was a collection of 51 pieces of prehistoric art, including an engraving of a mammoth on ivory, which had been found in 1864 by Lartet and Christy beneath a rocky overhang at La Madeleine near Les Eyzies. All over Paris people talked about it and the other examples of prehistoric art exhibited because the art obliged them to revise their hazy estimates of these primitive cave creatures. (One enthusiast offered a million francs for the collection.) Clearly, men capable of such controlled artistry could not be utter barbarians. But who were they? Where did they come from? What were they called?

These questions began to be answered a year later, thanks to the road workers of Les Eyzies. For the skeletons they uncovered in the rock shelter there belonged to the people who had shaped the lance heads and engraved the mammoth's tusk. They were the men who came to be called Cro-Magnon.

The advent of Cro-Magnon man, though he doubtless struck some 19th Century fundamentalists as a poor substitute for the Biblical Adam, was cordially regarded by many thoughtful people of the time. He testified to the principle of progress, just as Darwin's book seemed to testify, for some people, to the Grand Plan of the Universe, according to which life was evolving not aimlessly but towards nobler ends.

Optimism was catching. Some of it came from mechanical and scientific advances of the well-launched industrial age; it took shape in America in the Emersonian faith in the essential perfectibility of man. In England, Lord Tennyson voiced this faith disarmingly in his "In Memoriam":

> O, yet we trust that somehow good
>   Will be the final goal of ill,
>   To pangs of nature, sins of will,
> Defects of doubt, and taints of blood;

> That nothing walks with aimless feet;
>   That not one life shall be destroyed,
>   Or cast as rubbish to the void,
> When God hath made the pile complete.

This same optimism was reflected by the archaeological establishment. The French exhibition of prehistory in 1867 had been set up under the leadership of Edouard Lartet, but most of the work was done by Louis Laurent Marie Gabriel de Mortillet, a prehistorian who became a key figure in 19th Century archaeology. In the final sentence of the exhibit's guidebook, de Mortillet ringingly expressed the optimistic philosophy of the day: "The LAW OF HUMAN PROGRESS . . . and the GREAT ANTIQUITY OF MAN are . . . facts that emerge clearly, precisely and irrefutably from the study we have made of the Exhibition."

Considering the temper of the times, it is not surprising that an increasing number of young scientists were eager to uncover the piled-up evidence of prehistoric man, confident now that the final goal was worthy. Gradually archaeology became philosophically and even socially acceptable—one Oxford professor reported, with noticeable excitement, that many high-born young ladies, including duchesses and countesses, were attending his lectures.

Cro-Magnon man's appearance on the scene contributed a great deal to this philosophical acceptance of man's prehistory, but it also raised at the same time some vexing questions: Where did Cro-Magnon fit in the overall scheme of man's development? Had he lived elsewhere on earth, or only in those favoured valleys of the Dordogne? And, most difficult of all, where had he come from? From the Garden of Eden? From the apes of Africa? From some distant place in the mysterious East?

A great deal has been learned since those early days, but even now the answers are far from being final. The question of where Cro-Magnon man came from, for one thing, is still among the most absorbing and fascinating puzzles of the whole story of the emergence of man, one that archaeologists around the world are busily trying to solve.

A Rich Life: Creative, Inventive and Reverent

Assisted by an apprentice holding an oil lamp and another preparing pigments, a Cro-Magnon artist paints a horse on a cave wall.

Cro-Magnon man was a cave man with a difference. Underneath his unkempt exterior, he was a creature of intelligence and complexity, an innovative technician, a music maker and, above all, an artist. The tools that he fashioned were more finely made, more specialized and much more varied than those of his predecessors; his clothes were better tailored and decorated to please the eye; and the walls of his caves were painted and etched with art works that rank among the most elegant and captivating that man has ever produced.

Much of what is known about Cro-Magnons comes from evidence uncovered in the numerous caves and rock shelters of southwestern France; this evidence, analysed and pondered over by generations of archaeologists, gives a revealing glimpse of the rich life led by the last of the early men, the first of the modern men.

Surer Kills with New Weapons

Probably as skilful as any hunters who ever lived, the Cro-Magnons gained greater mastery over their prey because they took advantage not only of a fully developed intelligence but also of an effective new invention —the spear thrower. A simple rod about a foot long, hooked at one end to engage the butt of the spear, it enabled hunters like the three at right to hurl their weapons with much greater velocity—and therefore killing power —than hand-throwing could provide. Moreover, it permitted them to do so from a safe distance, out of range of hoofs and sharp teeth.

Most spear throwers were probably made out of wood, but the oldest ones to survive—all from Western Europe —are of reindeer antler. Among them are many with elaborate carved decorations, striking evidence that the Cro-Magnons' eye for beauty extended even to utilitarian objects.

Using spear throwers, rodlike devices made of reindeer antler, three hunters attack a herd of migratin

reindeer. From their kill they will get meat, hides and materials for tools to take to their home in a rock shelter in the cliff in the background.

Everyday Comforts from Fine Tools

Their superb craftsmanship in stone, bone, wood and antler gave the Cro-Magnons many kinds of efficient tools, with which they fashioned a better life for themselves. In addition to making powerful weapons that increased their kills of game, they devised scrapers, cutters, pointed burins and sewing needles that enabled them to make comfortable clothing, jewellery, snug shelters and many other necessities and luxuries.

In this domestic scene, a master stoneworker (*far right*) displays his skill, shaping tools from a piece of flint as two youths watch attentively to learn, one helping by holding the flint steady. On the left, a woman stitches together a garment of dressed hides with a needle made from reindeer antler, while a second woman behind her cleans the hide of a freshly killed reindeer with a flint scraper. Lining the rear wall of the rock shelter is a tentlike structure made of hides draped over poles, in which the band slept at night.

Facing south, the rock shelter inhabited by a band of Cro-Magnon hunter-gatherers captures the light

and warmth of the sun. When the weather grew damp or cold, the hide tent in the background, its floor covered with skins, would offer comfort.

In a cave's deepest recess, elders supervise an initiation rite that confers the privileges and duties of adulthood on six boys. An essential part of

...he ceremony is the frightening passage through dark tunnels to reach the sacred painted chamber.

Honouring Spirits in a Sacred Chamber

The evidence of the caves—painted and sculptured animals and abstract markings on walls and ceilings, many of them in hard-to-reach recesses —has convinced many experts that Cro-Magnons engaged in magic and ritual. Still at the mercy of nature, they apparently sought to influence it by appeals to supernatural powers —perhaps in the form of mystical ceremonies staged in the caverns' awe-inspiring settings.

One of the most important of such ceremonies observed among hunting peoples of modern times—on which the picture at left is based—is the initiation rite. In this ritual, boys at puberty are introduced to the spirits that will guide and protect them in adult life. In this scene a shaman, or sorcerer, wearing the skin and head of a bison, perhaps in mystical identification with the animal, plays a carved bone flute—one of the first musical instruments ever created. Two other men chant and beat rhythms on the cave floor with their hands.

In the dim torchlight the youthful initiates march, shirtless and grave, round and round in a circle, leaving in the damp earth heel marks that archaeologists would come across 15,000 years later—a cryptic suggestion of man's early attempts to cope with the spiritual meaning of life.

Chapter Two: A Citizen of the World

When the first skeletons of Cro-Magnon man were discovered, no one had the slightest idea how numerous his kind would turn out to be, or how significant his accomplishments actually were as he spread over the world and learned to prosper in all its environments. Even so, the finds were a sensation, for they seemed to settle some troubling questions about human origins.

The Cro-Magnon peoples were clearly ancestors of modern man. Equally clearly, they had lived long enough ago to have used stone tools and killed animals unknown in modern times. Yet they did not seem so ancient or so different from humans of later days as to cause any serious conflict with Biblical accounts of mankind.

Chauvinistic French experts were certain that Cro-Magnon man had arisen where his remains were first found, in France, and were almost prepared to place the Garden of Eden in the Vézère Valley. Others thought that he had originated in man's traditional birthplace, the Middle East, and migrated west. One eastward-looking anthropologist, explaining the rise of man from cave-dwelling crudity to Victorian perfection, believed that the Middle East was the place where humans had passed from the three stages of Savagery (Lower, Middle and Upper) through the three stages of Barbarism (Lower, Middle and Upper) into the enlightened stage of Civilization.

The skeleton of a Cro-Magnon man lies just as the body was buried 23,000 years ago in an ochre-sprinkled grave at Sungir, 130 miles east of Moscow. The man was ceremoniously laid to rest, laden with beads, bracelets and a headband of carved mammoth ivory and the teeth of arctic foxes, in what appears to have been a burial ground—suggesting that the hunter-gatherers of Sungir lived at least part of the year in a settled community where they developed complex customs.

Even the exponents of the new ideas of evolution, like their more conservative colleagues, speculated about where Cro-Magnon man had originated but tended to shy away from suggesting specifically how he might have evolved from his predecessors. There was as yet no evidence to connect him directly with any of the still older alleged ape-men or man-apes that had already begun to turn up in Europe. These creatures, actually Neanderthals, had many human characteristics, but their skulls—particularly the bony facial structures—made them look, to many mid-19th Century archaeologists, much more like apes than men. They appeared to be very distant relatives, evolutionary dead ends that were not in the direct line of human descent. That any of them could have evolved into modern man seemed incredible to most of the experts of the period.

And so, although some problems appeared solved, the essential mystery surrounding human origins remained. Modern man might indeed be the offspring of Cro-Magnon man. But, if this was the case, from whom was Cro-Magnon descended? The first hints of an answer to this crucial question showed up in 1931, when unusual fossils were found in the Skhul Cave on Mount Carmel, Israel, near Haifa. They turned out to share some of the archaic characteristics of Neanderthal man, who disappeared about 35,000 to 40,000 years ago, plus some of the more modern characteristics of Cro-Magnon man, who appeared at roughly the same time. Evidently these fossils represented either hybrids of Neanderthal and Cro-Magnon, or a people caught red-handed climbing the evolutionary ladder.

The implications of the Skhul discoveries were not generally accepted until the 1960s. But today most authorities believe that by about 40,000 years ago Neanderthal peoples in many parts of the world evolved into an assortment of Cro-Magnon-related types, all Homo sapiens sapiens—modern man. Oddly, the one place where transitional fossils have not been found is in southwestern France, home of the original Cro-Magnons. These peoples seem to bear little resemblance to Neanderthals, who lived near by; it has been suggested they may have migrated to France and replaced the more primitive indigenous peoples. Where did they come from? Quite possibly the Middle East —perhaps even the area where the Skhul fossils were found. But now no one knows for sure. The broad outlines of human origins, however, can finally be traced. Today, some two million years after the first man appeared on earth, his evolution can be seen to proceed from the last of the prehumans, Australopithecus, to the first human, Homo erectus, and from Homo erectus to Homo sapiens, the species that includes Neanderthal, Cro-Magnon and ourselves.

In the years since the first discovery of Cro-Magnon fossils, the skeletal remains of modern man have been turning up all over the world—in Hungary, in the U.S.S.R., in the Middle East and North Africa, as well as in South Africa, China and Southeast Asia, and even Australia and North America. Not all of the fossils are complete, of course, and some are no more than fragments, but everywhere they are what scientists call anatomically modern. For one thing, their bones are frequently lighter than those of their predecessors. For another, the Cro-Magnon skull is uniformly like the skulls of men living today: it has a definite chin, a high forehead, small teeth, a cranial capacity equal to that of its modern counterpart, and

it displays—for the first time—the necessary physical equipment for constructing complex and elaborate patterns of speech.

According to linguist Philip Lieberman of the University of Connecticut and anatomist Edmund S. Crelin of Yale University, who have studied the subject intensively, the arrangement of Cro-Magnon man's oral and nasal cavities, his longer pharynx— the section of throat just above the vocal cords —and the flexibility of his tongue enabled him to shape and project sounds over a much wider range, and much more rapidly, than early humans could. His superior vocalizing powers were gained at one big expense, however: modern man is the only creature who can choke to death on food caught in his windpipe, because his longer pharynx must do double duty as the route to his alimentary canal.

Although anatomically modern everywhere he lived, Cro-Magnon man's body was by no means everywhere the same. His bones in the Soviet Union were different from his bones in France, or in Africa or China, and they might be different from one site to another within a single region. Some anthropologists think that Cro-Magnon man may have come in more different varieties than his modern descendants; because his population was less mobile, it was less homogeneous, and groups thus tended to preserve their special traits. At the very outset this degree of variation among peoples of Cro-Magnon times misled scientists. Although bones are no clue to the colour of skin or the texture of hair, the temptation to flesh out the skeletons, so to speak, was irresistible— and some strange ideas sprang up.

Until well into the 20th Century, for instance, many experts believed that they had found the immediate ancestors of modern Negroes and Eskimos living side by side in southern Europe. The Grimaldi "Negro" fossils, found in a cave on the Italian Riviera, were so identified mainly because their lower faces—their upper and lower jaws—projected like those of some modern Negroes, but the projection later turned out to be distorted because of the way the fossils had been buried. The single "Eskimo" man, found near Chancelade, France, was classified on the basis of his wide cheekbones and heavy lower jaw. But anthropologists realized by the 1930s that these characteristics were also typical of many other peoples. And according to one report, the man who reassembled the Chancelade skeleton put the nasal bones in the wrong way round.

Until the mistake was discovered, however, modern Eskimos were believed by some people to have originated in southern France and to have followed the retreating glaciers northwards and eastwards across Europe into Siberia and ultimately across the Bering Strait into frigid regions of North America —surely one of the longest treks of all time.

Though the Italian Negroes and French Eskimos turned out to be mistakes, the fact remained that Cro-Magnon looked different in different places. Like men living today, he developed characteristic physical types from region to region, and even from site to site within a single region. The nature of his environment—its climate, its food supply—accounted for some of these variations. Such physical characteristics as tallness and shortness, dark skin and light skin, straight hair and curly hair, were formed during the millennia when man's body had to accommodate itself to heat and cold, and to the variations of sunlight in different latitudes. The relatively short,

thick bodies of the Eskimos, for instance, conserve heat better than the tall, thin bodies of some African Negroes, which present a much greater area of skin to be cooled by the air. Similarly, long straight hair and heavy beards, in the opinion of physical anthropologist Bernard Campbell of U.C.L.A., might help to husband body heat in cold climates, while tightly curled hair seems an adaptation guarding against tropical sunshine—it is a noticeable characteristic of genetically unrelated peoples in Africa and the islands of the South Pacific.

But by Cro-Magnon times many of the physical changes wrought by environment had largely been completed. The fact that Cro-Magnon peoples varied so widely in physical type from one location to another is apparently related more to demography than geography—to a great increase in numbers of people and to the division of the larger population into many isolated groups. The population growth expanded the "gene pool", the body of genetic material available to an entire species. At the same time, the isolated groups broke up the gene pool among small breeding populations, in some cases inhibiting "gene flow", the exchange of hereditary characteristics between groups of people.

When the total population of a species is relatively small, the genetic material available to it is relatively limited in scope, and the variant physical types may be few. But as the population increases, it also begins to vary, simply because greater numbers provide more opportunities for mutations, or variations, to appear. The variations become specialized, adapting to local environments when gene flow is limited. This specialization arises of course from natural selection—the tendency of certain traits to become

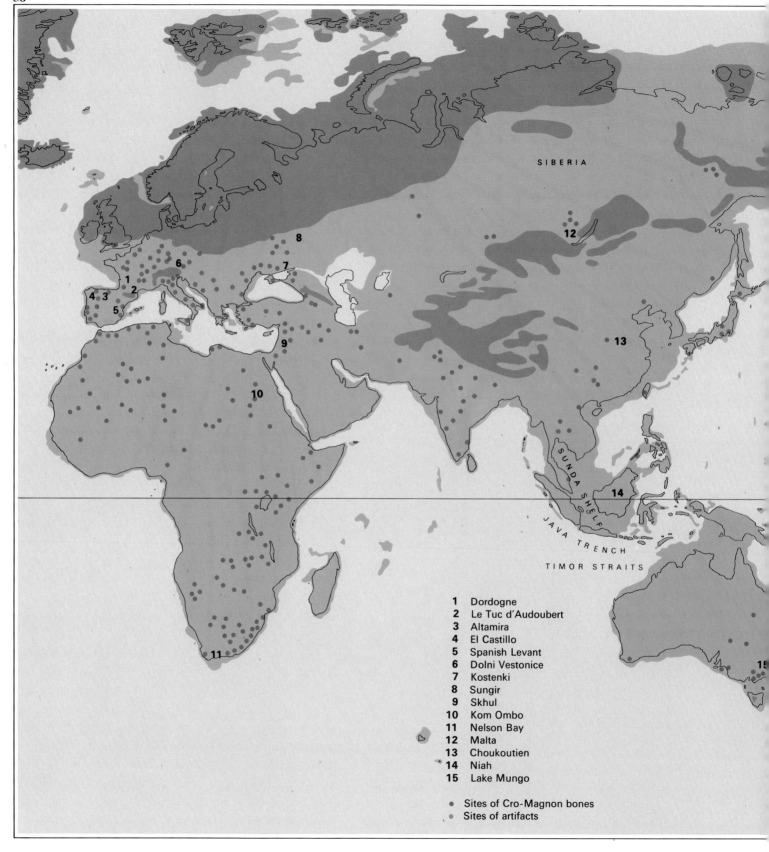

SIBERIA

12

13

SUNDA SHELF

14

JAVA TRENCH

TIMOR STRAITS

8

6
1
7
2
4 **3**
5
9

10

11

15

1	Dordogne
2	Le Tuc d'Audoubert
3	Altamira
4	El Castillo
5	Spanish Levant
6	Dolni Vestonice
7	Kostenki
8	Sungir
9	Skhul
10	Kom Ombo
11	Nelson Bay
12	Malta
13	Choukoutien
14	Niah
15	Lake Mungo

● Sites of Cro-Magnon bones
● Sites of artifacts

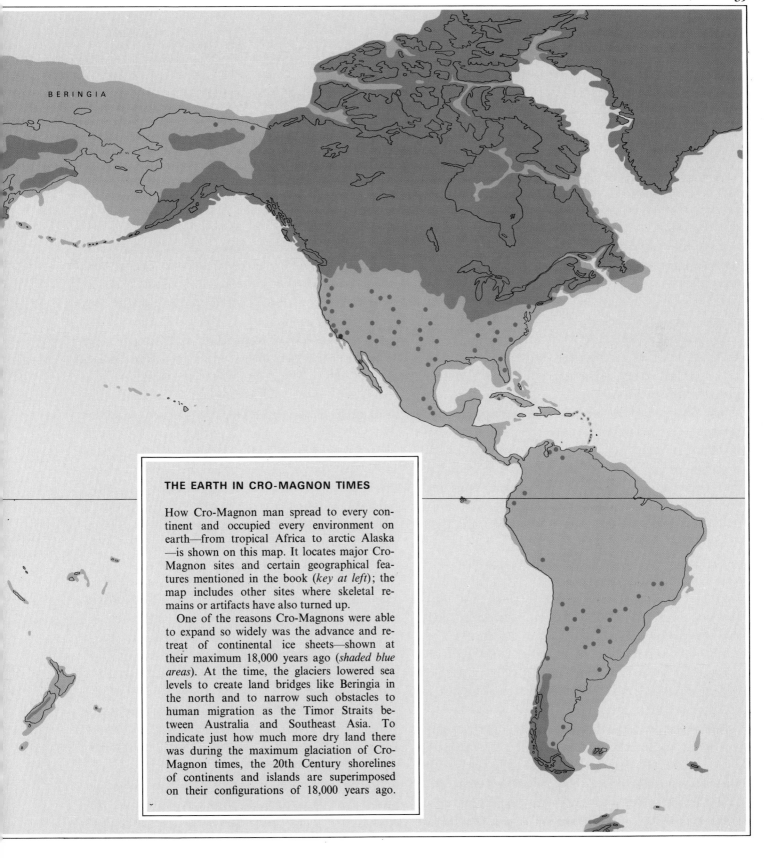

BERINGIA

THE EARTH IN CRO-MAGNON TIMES

How Cro-Magnon man spread to every continent and occupied every environment on earth—from tropical Africa to arctic Alaska —is shown on this map. It locates major Cro-Magnon sites and certain geographical features mentioned in the book (*key at left*); the map includes other sites where skeletal remains or artifacts have also turned up.

One of the reasons Cro-Magnons were able to expand so widely was the advance and retreat of continental ice sheets—shown at their maximum 18,000 years ago (*shaded blue areas*). At the time, the glaciers lowered sea levels to create land bridges like Beringia in the north and to narrow such obstacles to human migration as the Timor Straits between Australia and Southeast Asia. To indicate just how much more dry land there was during the maximum glaciation of Cro-Magnon times, the 20th Century shorelines of continents and islands are superimposed on their configurations of 18,000 years ago.

dominant or to recede, depending upon how well they fit the human animal for survival in a particular set of circumstances. In this process, the specialization is often influenced by what anthropologists call the founder effect. No newly founded breeding population takes with it the full genetic complement of its parent group—it retains only part of the original gene pool—and so its hereditary traits move off in a slightly different direction from the parent group. After scores of generations, members of the split-off group may bear little or no resemblance to the people who were their distant ancestors.

The reverse process is also in constant operation. Separate groups unite or, more commonly, foreign mates are brought into a group. Either way, gene flow is enhanced and new characteristics are introduced into the breeding population. Through such constant flowing of genetic material Cro-Magnon man gradually developed all the variant physical traits that exist in man today.

At the same time, along with this biological evolution, Cro-Magnon man was also evolving culturally. And here his progress is easier to trace. Cultural changes occur more rapidly than biological ones, and they leave behind numerous kinds of evidence. Habitation sites and the remains of the paraphernalia of living tell a great deal about how effectively people were using their bodies and their brains at a particular stage in their development.

Man was already well rooted in many parts of the world, for instance, when Cro-Magnon man arrived on the scene. He had moved out of the easy life of the tropics into the brisker climate of the Temperate Zone. From Africa and Southeast Asia he had migrated northwards into Europe and China. But there were still plenty of places in the world where he had not set foot—Siberia, the Arctic, the continent of Australia, the whole vast length and breadth of the New World. Cro-Magnon man moved into all four. Largely through his own capacity to change and adapt, and partly with the help of climatic changes, he took over every part of the globe that it is possible for man to inhabit.

Cro-Magnon lived towards the end of the ice age, technically the Würm/Wisconsin glaciation. Warm periods and cold ones followed one another in close succession—close at least by geological time—and with each climatic interlude the glaciers advanced and withdrew. If the earth's surface could have been viewed from a spacecraft at this time, it would have looked like the variegated surface of a giant soap bubble. Speed up the action as in time-lapse photography, so that thousands of years swirl by in a minute, and silvery-white ice fields would slide forth like spilled mercury, only to be replaced by unrolling carpets of green vegetation. Shorelines would waver and ripple like banners in a breeze as the oceans' shifting blues blanketed and then uncovered them. Islands would rise and fall like stepping stones, and natural causeways and conduits would appear, making new traffic routes for the comings and goings of man. Along one of these ancient routes Cro-Magnon man may have moved northwards from what is now China into the chilly reaches of Siberia. Along another one he apparently migrated from Siberia, across the dry land bridge of Beringia, now the Bering Sea, into the continent of North America.

But climatic alterations seem to have played no part in his migration to Australia. Although the vast icecaps of the last glaciation locked up enough of the world's water to drop sea levels as much as 400 feet, adding great expanses of dry land to the continents, such extensions never joined Australia to the mainland of Southeast Asia. Waters subsiding from the comparatively shallow Sunda Shelf united Borneo, Java and Sumatra, and probably exposed enough small islands to make island-hopping feasible. But between Australia and the shelf at the edge of the Asian mainland there still remained the 26,400-foot-deep waters of the Java Trench, 60 miles of open sea. How did men living as far back as Cro-Magnon times manage to get across it?

It was long assumed that man did not reach this major island continent until the ancestors of the modern aborigines migrated there by boat, probably from Southeast Asia, some 8,000 to 10,000 years ago. Seaworthy boats were presumably available at that time. Then in the 1930s finds indicated an earlier human arrival, and in 1968 archaeologists digging near Lake Mungo in New South Wales discovered a 27,000-year-old skeleton of a woman and artifacts dating back as far as 32,000 years—long before any archaeological evidence of the existence of boats. Yet the lonely lady was unmistakably modern in her anatomy, a true Homo sapiens.

Obviously people living more than 30,000 years ago somewhere in Southeast Asia must at this early date have invented some sort of watercraft. Was it simply a raft of bundled bamboo and reeds, meant for offshore fishing? Or was it perhaps a primitive version of the dugout canoe used today by modern Melanesians? Even more intriguing is the question of how the voyagers happened to journey to Australia. Were they carried there inadvertently by a wayward current or, according to one far-out speculation, by a

Puzzling marks, scratched on the walls of Australia's Koonalda Cave 20,000 years ago, are believed to be evidence of a rite conducted by early settlers of the island continent as they mined the cave for chunks of flint to use in manufacturing tools. Most of these markings were made with the fingertips in soft sandstone (top); others were incised in harder rock with stone chips.

massive tidal wave like the one that rolled out from the island of Krakatoa during a volcanic eruption there in the 19th Century? Did they go to Australia on purpose, and if so, what drew them?

No one believes that exploration per se was Cro-Magnon man's forte, nor was it his main cultural accomplishment. Like the migrations of all the hunting and gathering peoples who had gone before him, his movements were concerned with getting food. In the means he used to achieve this end—in his implements, his techniques, his social organization, his choice of habitation—he went far beyond what anyone had done before. His diet included every sort of food the earth provided, and he became enormously adept at acquiring it. Indeed, in terms of living off the land, and living well, Cro-Magnon man may have been far more successful than anyone before his time or at any time since.

When the first men developed their skills as hunters, they tapped a source of food energy unavailable to vegetarian predecessors. The nutrients contained in meat were, in part at least, acquired from plant material man himself could not eat. When he began to hunt migratory grazing animals—and an occasional predatory animal whose territory extended beyond his own—his intake of food energy began to draw upon a still-wider range of resources, for these animals got their food outside man's own environment. And when his territorial expansion took him into the Temperate Zone, where grazing herd animals some-

Carved from mammoth ivory, this small, stylized figure of a waterfowl in flight suggests the concern of the ancient hunters of Siberia with migratory birds and mammals, a major source of their food. All of the many bird figurines unearthed there have flattened bodies, elongated necks and short wings.

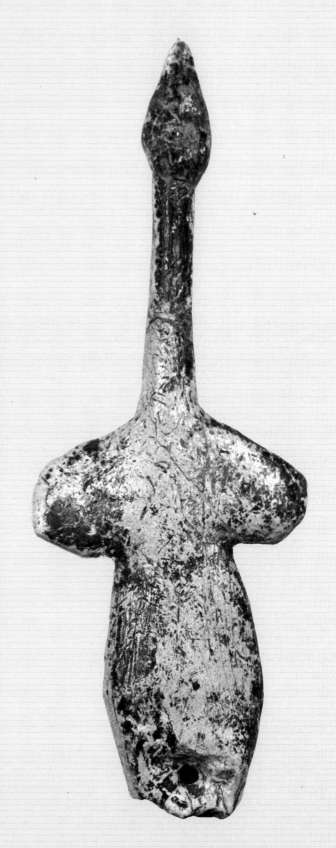

times migrate between winter and summer feeding grounds, man's food intake tapped nutritional energy from sources at some distance, and sometimes extremely different, from those supplied by his own immediate environment. Neanderthal man, harvesting the reindeer of the Dordogne region, was benefiting from the nutrients of the northern pastures and coastal plains where the reindeer herds did some of their grazing, but where he himself seldom, if ever, ventured. Scientists call this kind of long-distance food collection "living on unearned resources". Of all the ways in which organisms had adapted to and drawn sustenance from their environment short of actually controlling it, it was the most sophisticated. Not until agriculture was developed did man's exploitation of nature become more complex.

By the time Cro-Magnon man arrived on the earth, men were already using the unearned resources of migratory animals to supplement a diet of plant foods. Cro-Magnon man did it far more efficiently. With his quicker wits and his better weapons, he harvested animals in such abundance that it became possible for him to survive in the Arctic, where plant foods are so scarce that almost all human food resources are unearned. All across Siberia, from the river Yenisei Valley in the west to the Kamchatka Peninsula in the far east, Soviet archaeologists are uncovering in more than a dozen sites the evidence of human habitation going back perhaps 30,000 years. Siberian winters were even longer and colder then than they are now, and there were few trees to break the fierce winds that drove across the miles and miles of open steppes. Three feet down, the ground was permanently frozen, discouraging any sort of deep-rooted vegetation. But the top layer of soil supported the sturdy grasses and low-growing shrubs that make perfect grazing for herd animals.

Siberia, in fact, was a paradise for hunters, and Cro-Magnon man prospered in it, despite the cold. The refuse heaps outside his habitation sites are thick with the bones of reindeer, wild horse, antelope, mammoth and bison, and on rare occasions he apparently even took on bear and lion. There are also the bones of fox and wolf, which may have been eaten but more likely were treasured for their thick, warm pelts, which the Siberians tailored into clothing. And, finally, at several of these Siberian sites the refuse heaps contain evidence of two new food sources that other Cro-Magnon peoples were also occasionally tapping: birds and fish.

Fishing was probably a summer activity for these Siberian peoples, since the ice on the rivers would have been many feet deep in winter. And the birds they ate were primarily ptarmigan, which are ground-dwelling and slow-flying and relatively easy to catch. But some anthropologists think that they may also have gone after waterfowl occasionally. Perhaps they brought down the birds on the wing with well-aimed projectiles; perhaps they trapped them with snares similar to the kind still used by the Netsilik Eskimos north of Hudson Bay. This device is an ingenious arrangement of rawhide baited with fish and triggered with a carefully balanced stone; when the bird alights for the bait, the stone is dislodged and the rawhide thongs close around its legs, hobbling the bird and making it easy to capture and kill.

In so rigorous a land, where the winters were long and cruel, the Siberians must have led a far more carefully planned existence than the easy life of their tropical contemporaries. When the weather was at its worst, they settled into snug houses of skin with stone foundations sunk as much as 30 inches into the earth. In an almost equally rigorous environment in the Ukraine, similarly constituted houses were large enough to accommodate as many as 15 or 20 people. Tucked into frigid storage vaults behind the stone foundations was enough meat to last many days. Some of it was frozen, some of it had been dried in the sun or smoke-dried. In the cheering light of a circle of open hearths these people whiled away the dark days carving tools and ornaments of bone, exchanging hunting lore with friends, passing on knowledge to children. And when a member of their circle died, he was buried with love and affection. In a grave at a site called Malta, near the southern end of Lake Baikal, archaeologists found the skeleton of a four-year-old girl, decked with an ivory "diadem", an ivory bracelet and a necklace of 120 ivory beads. Near by were other objects of bone and stone, funeral gifts to a child from people who cherished her.

While these northernmost ancestors of modern man were learning to cope with a rugged climate, another group of Cro-Magnon peoples in an equable environment halfway around the world were adapting to a radical change in ecology. Nelson Bay Cave lies about 300 miles east of Cape Town, South Africa, along the Indian Ocean. It is carved into a 200-foot-high sandstone bluff about 65 feet up from the present beach, and it was inhabited continuously during Cro-Magnon times by a succession of peoples, beginning about 18,000 years ago. The cave opening faces south and is 100 feet wide; inside there is a spacious chamber roughly 30 feet high and 100 to 150 feet deep; a spring rises at the very back and has done so for more than 35,000 years, so the cave has always had a convenient supply of fresh water. As a dwelling place it offered so many natural advantages that there is no reason to wonder at its continuous occupation by 400 generations of hunters and gatherers—even when the food resources available to them outside the cave altered drastically.

For its first 6,000 years as a home for modern man, the cave overlooked an open grassland studded with low-growing trees, not unlike the modern African savanna. The sea lay as much as 50 miles away, and the Nelson Bay peoples rarely, if ever, went there: at this level the cave contains no fossil marine life of any kind. Instead, the early residents lived on what was close at hand. While the women collected seeds and berries and dug up roots and bulbs, the men hunted the game that roamed in abundance over the wide plain—antelopes, ostriches, baboons, and such now-extinct species as the giant buffalo, weighing 3,500 pounds, and an equally outsized hartebeest that was the size of a modern Percheron horse. They also went after bush pigs and wart hogs, mean-tempered beasts with fearsome tusks, which travel in packs and are tricky to hunt. When pursued, these wild hogs turn en masse on their pursuers.

During this period the Nelson Bay Cave may have been occupied year round except for occasional hunting forays. To make the cave more homelike, its occupants added certain refinements. They encircled their hearths with stones and may have built a semicircular windbreak between the hearths and the mouth of the cave—the postholes for a somewhat later windbreak are still there. The covering could have been animal skins or brushwood or a palisade of saplings. In winter, and especially at night, this windbreak would have been comforting, for the climate of South Africa was cooler then than now, and moist, rather like the climate of Seattle, Washington. Outside the cave there might have been frost, and even a light dusting of snow.

Beginning around 12,000 years ago this life style changed, suddenly and dramatically in terms of geological time. The world's climate, which had gradually been warming for 4,000 to 5,000 years, had melted enough of the glacier ice to raise the sea level above the shelf that marked the end of the 50-mile-long Nelson Bay plain. Almost like a river in flood that overflows its banks and spreads quickly over the low-lying countryside, the sea moved relatively rapidly up the shallow slope of the plain and was soon breaking just a few miles away from the base of the cliff where the cave was situated. With their former grazing land now underwater, the animals naturally moved inland, and it would have been just as natural for the Nelson Bay peoples to do the same, reestablishing themselves elsewhere.

But they did not. For some reason, perhaps some Stone Age feeling for "home", the cave continued to be a base of operations, though not one that was lived in year round. In summer the inhabitants went off on extended hunting trips, tracking and killing the game, collecting the bulbs, berries and seeds that had formed their traditional food supply in centuries past. In winter, however, they returned to the Nelson Bay Cave to harvest another source of energy: food taken from the sea.

Instead of gathering seeds and digging up roots, the women now scavenged for limpets and abalone in the wake of the receding tide (*pages 74-75*), prying them from the surfaces of rocks in tidal pools and deeper waters. To aid them in this task they had a nine-inch flat bone knife and probably some sort of carrying container, a basket or leather pouch, into which they dropped their catches. So dexterous did they become at this new form of food collecting that archaeologists have found piles of discarded marine shells as much as 20 feet deep. The fishy residue of this midden must have smelled to high heaven—reason enough for these later Nelson Bay peoples to leave home periodically, as some present-day aborigines do when their kitchen refuse gets out of hand. In the cave dwellers' seasonal absence, rodents, sea birds and the scouring sea winds would have cleaned up the stinking mess.

While the women harvested shellfish, the men of Nelson Bay went fishing or walked several miles up the beach to a rocky outcropping that had become a breeding ground for Cape fur seals. It takes no great skill to kill a seal in a rookery, where the animals congregate by the thousands. The Nelson Bay hunters probably used the same tactics as 20th Century seal hunters, wading among the furry hordes and hitting the animals over the head with heavy clubs. Seals added still another unearned food resource to the Cro-Magnon diet: in the summer months the Cape fur seal feeds on small fish and squid several hundred miles offshore.

Possibly the seal hunters were also acquiring more than a new source of food. Eskimos, whose economy depends to a large extent on seals, use the fat of the animals for their oil lamps, their sinews for sewing thread and bindings, and their waterproof coats for clothing, storage bags and even for boats—the Eskimo kayak is made of sealskin stretched over a wood or bone frame. The Nelson Bay peoples may not have explored all these potentials. They would not, for instance, have needed the Eskimos' tailored sealskin clothing, and though they lived along the sea, they were probably not tempted to venture onto it in any sort of boat—the surf near Nelson Bay is high and rough, known to surfers the world over for its big waves. But seal oil burning in stone lamps could very well have supplemented firelight in the Nelson Bay Cave as a source of illumination. And among the many uses they could have found for the seal's tough sinews, one very possibly was fishing line.

The Nelson Bay peoples are known to have caught at least four kinds of fish. One of the fish fossils in their cave has been identified as a mussel cracker, a big-toothed creature that still frequents the same waters and comes in close to shore to bite mussels from rocks for its food. It could have been hooked on a fishing line baited with mussel and a carved bone or wood fish gorge, one of Cro-Magnon man's newly invented tools (*Chapter Three*).

For the Nelson Bay peoples life settled into a routine of food-gathering that took them at regular intervals from one environment to the other, from the coast to the interior, and from a diet composed primarily of seafoods to one that combined the traditional inland meat and plant foods. But 4,500 miles away, along the Nile, lived another community of Cro-Magnon peoples who could enjoy all this food variety without leaving home—and so they stayed.

Beginning around 17,000 years ago and for a period of about 5,000 years—until some climatic change, perhaps a drought, altered their life style —groups of people with at least five different tool kits settled down in the wide Kom Ombo Plain, 28 miles downriver from the present Aswan Dam, and took the step that a few thousand years later would

Enlarged portion in box

A limpet shell from a cave in South Africa (top) has been sawed in two to be studied by physicists. Into the edge of the shell's outermost layers (boxed section, shown enlarged in lower picture)—the last layers added before the animal died —tiny holes are drilled to produce dust for analysis. A machine called a mass spectrometer then analyses the dust to determine the ratio of two types of oxygen—0-18 and 0-16 —contained in the shell. Since a relatively high proportion of 0-18 is characteristic of cold sea water, scientists assume that high 0-18 in a shell such as this one indicates that the animal had its last growth in winter, just before a forager ate it.

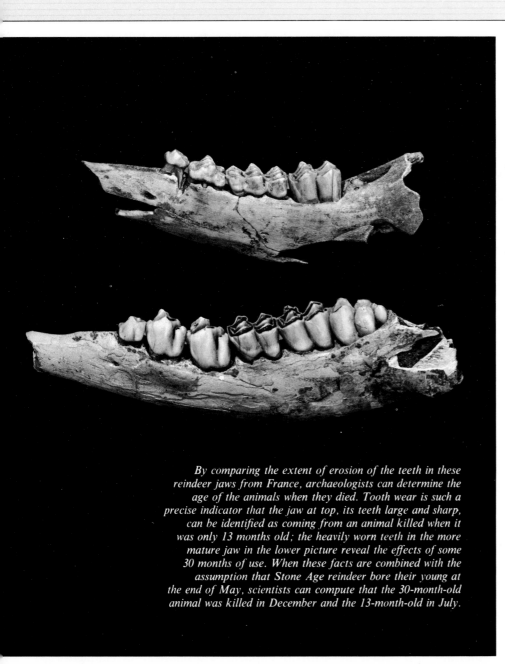

By comparing the extent of erosion of the teeth in these reindeer jaws from France, archaeologists can determine the age of the animals when they died. Tooth wear is such a precise indicator that the jaw at top, its teeth large and sharp, can be identified as coming from an animal killed when it was only 13 months old; the heavily worn teeth in the more mature jaw in the lower picture reveal the effects of some 30 months of use. When these facts are combined with the assumption that Stone Age reindeer bore their young at the end of May, scientists can compute that the 30-month-old animal was killed in December and the 13-month-old in July.

Clues to Man's Seasonal Activities 30,000 Years Ago

Archaeologists, in their efforts to glean every clue that might shed some light on prehistoric ways of life, fine-comb Cro-Magnon man's trash—with some illuminating results. The two types of animal remains pictured at left— French reindeer jawbones and a portion of a South African limpet shell —were found in caves, rock shelters and other sites where Cro-Magnon people once lived; both the bones and the shells were undoubtedly refuse from meals. But in recent decades, physical and biological analyses of this ancient garbage have helped some archaeologists to convert it into a calendar of the past that tells a great deal about the eating and hunting habits of Cro-Magnons.

The limpets reveal in their chemical composition that they were invariably gathered in winter, the time of year when other food was in short supply, and when shellfish, probably free of the effects of the poisonous red tides caused in the summer by algae, could safely be eaten. But reindeer seem, from studies of their tooth-wear patterns, to have been killed and consumed all year long.

lead to farming. They became intensive foragers, gathering enough of a few types of plants and animals so that they could settle in one place and live year round on their specialized foods. If they did not actually plant grain, they harvested the seeds of wild grasses systematically and efficiently.

Then as now, the Kom Ombo Plain stretched inland from the east bank of the Nile in a flat oval that covered some 248 square miles, the largest such plain in Upper Egypt. It was formed by two wadis—beds of seasonal rivers—that originated in the mountains beyond the eastern desert along the west coast of the Red Sea, and it was crisscrossed with channels of the Nile that ran full from August through October, swelled by the monsoon rains that fell on East Africa and fed the river's headwaters. From March to August the Kom Ombo Plain had a dry spell, though probably it was not as dry as now, for the North African climate 17,000 years ago was generally cooler and wetter than it is today.

These seasonal changes brought into the plain a constantly changing succession of wildlife. Wild cattle, which like to be near water, grazed over the area when the streams were full and the grasses young and succulent. Gazelles and hartebeests moved in during the dry season when the vegetation was more like that of their regular habitat, the savanna. When the river and streams were high, there were catfish, perch, soft-shelled Nile turtle and hippopotamus to be caught. And all through the year there were water birds of many kinds, some of them local, some of them annual migrants from the cold European winter. Archaeologists digging in the sites occupied by the various Kom Ombo hunter-gatherer groups have come upon the bones of ducks, geese, cormorants,

herons, mergansers, ospreys, eagles, cranes and curlews. Supporting this concentration of varied wildlife, large portions of the plain were covered with thick stands of cereal grasses that may have been related to such grains as sorghum and barley.

Not surprisingly, Kom Ombo's varied food supply, its streams and its spacious meadowlands attracted many people to the area. Archaeologists think that the plain may have supported as many as 150 to 200 people at a time. At nearly one person per square mile, that would have amounted in Stone Age terms to crowding. And it seems to have produced some interesting results. Clustered in enclaves along the banks of the many streams, each group of people —numbering perhaps about 25 or 30—developed its own distinctive style of living. Sometimes the communal "trademark" was a particular kind of tool, sometimes it was a particular technique for food-gathering. Competition may have driven the groups into some of these forms of specialization, but in a world suddenly grown populous, perhaps men were seeking to establish some sort of social order, a sense of group identity.

Some of the most fascinating of these group specializations were practised by peoples who were more interested in grains than any of their predecessors on the plain had been. They harvested and processed the wild grains with such intensity that a good part of their nutritional needs may have been met by grain alone. Among the artifacts of these gathering peoples are stone sickles and massive grinding stones (*page 49*). The stones are slightly concave in the centre, forming a trough for the grain, and they are accompanied by disc-shaped rubbing stones. Together they form an implement rather like the metate

A grooved 10-pound grindstone and a crude pestle attest to the adaptability of hunting societies in North Africa's Kom Ombo areas towards the end of the ice age. About 17,000 years ago, population pressure drove some groups to seek additional food sources from their environment. Abundant wild grains, milled with tools like these, became an important part of their diet. But some 5,000 years later, when the supply of grains was appreciably reduced, possibly by a long dry period, the groups concentrated again on hunting.

and mano combination that Indians of the American Southwest use to grind their corn.

The Kom Ombo grindstones are found along the lower slopes of the sandstone cliffs from which they were originally collected, and there are usually a number of them together. Archaeologists think that the grinding task may have been a group activity and that probably the grain harvest was, too. As the heads of the grasses ripened, the band would converge on each stand en masse, hand-stripping the seeds or cutting the stalks with stone sickles, and carrying the grain to the site of the grinding stones for threshing —possibly underfoot—and "milling".

Except for the sickles and grinding stones, however, none of the artifacts of the entire harvesting process remain. Did the Kom Ombo peoples thresh the grain with bundled sticks, as primitive farmers still do today? Did they free it of what little chaff it may have had by tossing it in the air on a windy day? And what sort of container did they use to transport the grain to the "mill"? Drawing upon the Nile's abundant supply of reeds and grasses, the successors to these Stone Age peoples became skilful basket-makers. Did the earlier Nile people try their hand at weaving and construct a kind of mat or tray on which to pile the grain?

Even more intriguing, what did they do with the product? Presumably, they used it for porridge and for thickening meat stews. But the fact that they ground the grain into meal suggests that they also made some form of bread, perhaps an unleavened mixture of meal and water baked on a hot stone, as many present-day peoples do. Some scholars have even suggested that they may also have made beer from the grain.

In the fertile valleys of Egypt, on the frigid plains of Siberia, along the seacoast of Africa, Cro-Magnon man was demonstrating that he could not only stay alive but could actually prosper under conditions of extraordinary diversity. Cold was no barrier to his existence; when meat was scarce his food became fish; with foresight and planning he harvested entire crops of grain in one concerted operation. After centuries of being a nomad, of moving from place to place in pursuit of game or of fresh supplies of plant food, he was finally able to stay in one place and systematically exploit the seasonal resources of one locality. He was, in short, becoming the master of the world he inhabited.

This change in his economic status inevitably produced profound changes in his physical well-being and mode of living. For one thing, Cro-Magnon man was probably healthier than his predecessors. With a sufficiency of food and a more rounded diet, he must have been stronger and more alert, better able to out-run and out-manœuvre many of the animals he hunted. Possibly, he also lived a bit longer, and the extra time on earth allowed him not only to accumulate more knowledge but to pass on more of his knowledge to his children and grandchildren.

Along with his better health, Cro-Magnon's efficiency as a food producer also gave him certain advantages. Since he was often able to lead a more sedentary life, he could acquire more material goods, objects that it would have been impractical for him to own as long as he was peripatetic. In several Cro-Magnon sites in central Europe, for instance, men were shaping objects from clay, and even firing them in dome-shaped kilns. But even more important than material wealth was the accumulation of technical and social knowledge that provided Cro-Magnon man with a base on which to build language, art and religion, and to develop the complex forms of social and political organization that are the hallmark of all fully developed human cultures.

A Surprising Way to Survive on the Steppes

Burdened with scavenged mammoth bones and tusks, five Kostenki men head for their winter camp in the valley of the river Don.

The seminomadic hunters who inhabited Russia's river Don Valley 20,000 years ago lived amid a paradoxical contrast of abundance and scarcity. On the one hand, huge herds of game roamed the grassy steppe, providing food and skins for clothing and shelter. On the other hand, wood, a crucial raw material for most Cro-Magnons, was scarce in the almost treeless permafrost landscape.

Rich finds excavated at Kostenki, a large prehistoric site some 290 miles southeast of Moscow, show how these people solved the problem. To compensate for the lack of wood, they collected the scattered bones of countless animals, many of them of mammoths. Through their ingenuity, the skeletons, tusks and antlers were converted into tools, weapons, sewing needles, statuettes, jewellery, even fuel —supporting, in short, a complex and comfortable existence.

Thirteen members of a band of some 100 hunters who have gathered for the winter ready a long house for the frigid months ahead. The onl

Storing Bones for Winter

As winter approaches, a band of Kostenki hunters prepares for a long stay in the river Don Valley at a spot favoured because it is well protected from fierce upland winds. Although it is only October, snow flurries have already dappled the ground.

For several years, the band has wintered here in communal long houses like this one—each a series of three tepee-like frames lashed together with rawhide and covered with the skins of big-game animals. Left unoccupied through the summer, while the band was hunting in the uplands, the long house is now in need of repairs. Two women sitting on the grass stitch together patches for the walls, as the men in the background hoist mammoth bones and tusks—some of which weigh as much as 100 pounds apiece—to pile around the base of the house and secure it firmly.

In the foreground, a man digs a storage pit for food and for bones and choice pieces of ivory, which during the winter months will be made into armbands like the one worn by the man at extreme right, or ornaments such as adorn the leather clothing of the man in the foreground. Supplies in the pit, covered over and weighted down by more of the huge bones, will be safe from scavenging animals.

person without a specific task, a young boy (foreground), imitates his father, who is digging a pit.

A Commune in a Long House

Heedless of the Russian winter's sub-zero weather outside, several families enjoy the security of warmth and camaraderie inside the long house they share. The focus of indoor life is the hearth, a shallow pit in which the fuel is either mammoth bone, hacked into small pieces, or dried dung. Leading to each hearth is a long groove dug into the ground to draw air under the flames and thus help burn the normally fire-resistant bone.

Because winter cuts hunting to a minimum, the men have plenty of leisure time. In this scene, they are swapping tales and playing a game of chance with thrown pieces of polished and decorated bone. The women, on the other hand, busy themselves with chores. One (*at far right*) sews hides together to make clothes for the children, menfolk and herself. At the end of the long house, another woman keeps watch over a chunk of horse-meat roasting on a mammoth-bone spit. One of the children, meanwhile, has found a fascinating toy in the form of a hollowed-out leg bone from a horse (*right foreground*).

Inside one of four hide-covered long houses at the winter settlement, several families share living

quarters only 30 feet long and eight feet wide; a larger house would be difficult to construct and to heat. Each family has its own living space.

Bundled in their warmest winter garb—fur boots and arctic fox parkas and trousers, snugly tailored with the fur side turned in to hold body hea

An Ancient Snare for Fur and Food

During the frigid winter days, almost nothing could draw the Kostenki men out of the comfort of their houses —except the need for fresh meat or fur. Winter, they knew, is the time of the year when the coats of wolves, arctic foxes and hares are at their bushiest. Several arctic fox pelts, properly cured and then stitched together, could make a garment that had no equal for warmth.

Here a father and son have come upon a fox dangling in a snare they have set. The trap—one of the oldest hunting devices known—consists of a rawhide noose attached at one end to a sapling. To set the snare, the attachment was pulled to bend the sapling, and looped over a bone held by a rock; the noose was laid on the snowy ground where the prey was expected to step. When the fox walked into the noose, it tripped the snare and pulled the loop off the bone; the sapling then sprang back and the tightened noose yanked the fox into the air.

—a father and son approach a snared fox. The man holds a mammoth bone ready to club the fox.

Harvesting Summer's Bounty

Spring promised a brief respite from cold weather at Kostenki, but also heralded hard work. Having left their riverside winter camp, these hunters have moved to the rolling uplands, where herds of big game habitually graze. In this windswept region only low grasses and shrubs grew, and thus the hunters could easily spot the horses, bison, antelope and reindeer on which they preyed.

Two hunters, at far right, have bagged a saiga antelope and are bringing it back to their encampment. Game killed earlier in the day is keeping the rest of the group busy. One woman has just finished cutting meat into narrow strips; she is now draping the strips over a leather line where they will dry, to be set aside as part of the group's winter food supply. Another is scraping bits of fat and flesh off a large hide pegged to the ground. When the skin is scraped clean, it will be treated, possibly with smoke, then stored away and, in a few months, used to reline one of the long houses standing unoccupied in the valley.

For their summer stay in the uplands, the band has separated into small groups of about three families

…ach to permit greater mobility in pursuing big game. Lean-tos that are easily collapsed for a quick move provide shelter from the continual wind.

Chapter Three: Stone Age Technology

A finely chipped "laurel leaf" blade from France, shown at left in full size and at far left in a close-up view, is so delicate it could have served no practical purpose. The blade—11 inches long, but only four tenths of an inch thick—may have been some sort of ceremonial object or even the proud emblem of a master toolmaker.

Someday in the distant future, when the petrol engine is a quaint relic of the past, penicillin is regarded as a curious nostrum, and steel is obsolete, archaeologists may look back on the 20th Century and marvel that human beings with such limited technology managed to get on so well. In the same way, people today tend to imagine their Cro-Magnon ancestors as brutish creatures battering at mammoth carcasses with unwieldy, dull-edged chunks of rock, and wonder that such ill-equipped men could cope with their harsh, cold ice-age environment.

Just how distorted that image is becomes perfectly clear to anyone who has ever held in his hands and examined a Stone Age tool such as the magnificent "laurel leaf" blade on the opposite page. Its superb proportions and exquisite workmanship belie any notion of clumsy ineptitude on the part of the person who made it; instead they speak of an elegant technical achievement. For the truth is, Cro-Magnon man was a highly efficient and innovative toolmaker who accomplished one of the great leaps forward in the history of technology. During the 30,000 or so years of his tenure, he made more technological progress, and in the process gained more control over his environment, than men had managed in all the 1.3 million years of human experience before him.

He was the master stoneworker of all time, improving old techniques to produce tools of greater effectiveness and variety. But he also exploited other materials—bone, antler, ivory—that had been little used earlier, and with them he fashioned new weapons and new devices for employing them efficiently, as well as domestic inventions and decorative objects. He learned to build better fires more easily, and use them for new purposes. Some of the shelters he built were but a step away from real houses; they were more durable than earlier ones, and they afforded more protection against the elements—and when the climate changed, he invented ways to deal with it. Technological innovation and cultural adaptation replaced physical evolution, and man's links to his animal past were now beginning to be more and more behind him. He still depended on nature, but it no longer ruled him. From the tropics to the arctic he forged a notably successful relationship with nature and, by and large, his life around the world was a good one.

Improvement in his stone tools was crucial to Cro-Magnon man's new technical mastery, but it is ironic that no one really knows what purpose was served by the most beautiful examples of this new skill—fine blades like the 11-inch-long laurel leaf, so named for its shape. Too delicate for a knife, too big and fragile for a spear, so beautifully crafted a piece of flint seems to be a showpiece. Clearly, to produce an object of such daring proportions required craftsmanship bordering on art, and many archaeologists think this masterpiece and others like it may have been just that—works of art that served an aesthetic or ritual function rather than a utilitarian one and may even have been passed, as highly prized items, from one man or group to another.

If such large laurel leaves were made for no useful purpose, they were clearly then an instance of technology transcending itself, because the smaller, everyday implements on which such showpieces were modelled had strictly practical functions. Thousands of other stone points in various sizes have been found in excavations in western Europe, and there is no doubt that many of these could have served most effectively as spear points or knives with razor-sharp edges. They were basic items in the armoury of a people who, living and hunting in the game-rich countryside of Europe, depended for their existence less and less on the simple strength of their biceps and more and more on their brain power and the efficiency of their weapons.

The stone blades were unquestionably sharp and efficient. Modern experiments have shown that well-made flint projectile points of a similar type are sharper than iron points and penetrate more deeply into an animal's body. So flint knives are equal, if not superior, to steel knives in their cutting power. The only drawback of both is that, because of their brittleness, they break more easily and have to be replaced more often.

The vital rôle such tools played in the lives of Cro-Magnon hunters lends authority to the theory that the large, nonutilitarian examples—of which at least several dozen have been found—might have been ritualistic objects representing the quintessential spear point. On the other hand, it has also been suggested that a magnificent laurel leaf might have been simply a tour de force tossed off by a virtuoso toolmaker to demonstrate his talent. If so, any admiration or praise he received from his family, friends or group was well deserved. The laurel leaf is without doubt a splendid creation, and there are no more than a handful of people in the world today who are skilled enough in the ancient craft to produce one.

It is understandable, but perhaps a bit sad, that a skill so basic to man's existence for well over a million years should have become all but extinct in the past few centuries. There are a few hunter-gatherer peoples, such as the Australian aborigines, who still

make stone arrowheads, spear points and scrapers, but they are fast abandoning stone for the metals of the modern age. In mechanized society there are a few scattered companies of artisans who also practice the ancient art to one degree or another. Farmers in the village of Cakmak, in Turkey, for example, fashion rough flint blades for wood sledges that they drag over their wheat to thresh it. In Brandon, England, one or two craftsmen still make flints for flintlock guns to sell to Revolutionary War buffs in America. Finally, there are around the world a few amateur enthusiasts, mostly archaeologists, who have patiently taught themselves the fine points of flint knapping, as it is called, in order to learn more about how prehistoric man lived and to find out how he may have used his tools (for a demonstration of the technique by a Frenchman, see pages 83-91).

To master the craft is no easy matter. First of all, the knapper must know his stone—the raw material from which he will chip off pieces to be processed into tools. The best stones are those with a fine, even texture. In fact, one of the most easily worked substances of all is not even stone: it is glass. Glass insulators on the telegraph poles in the outback of Australia were taken faster than they could be replaced by stoneworking aborigines who prized them for making tools. The telegraph linemen finally took to leaving stacks of insulators at the base of the poles as offerings to the aborigines.

Glass is very brittle, however, and in its natural state, as obsidian or volcanic glass, it is rare. The next best thing is flint. Its fine crystalline texture allows the knapper to dictate the shape he will produce. In coarse stone like granite or layered stone like slate, flaws and a large granular structure make such con-

The periods during which the five major styles of tool manufacture flourished in France are indicated on this time chart. Each bar stands for a different style; a broken bar indicates uncertainty about when the style began or ended. The Solutrean and Magdalenian together represent a high point in Cro-Magnon technology. The Azilian, which followed, disappeared shortly before the rise of agriculture.

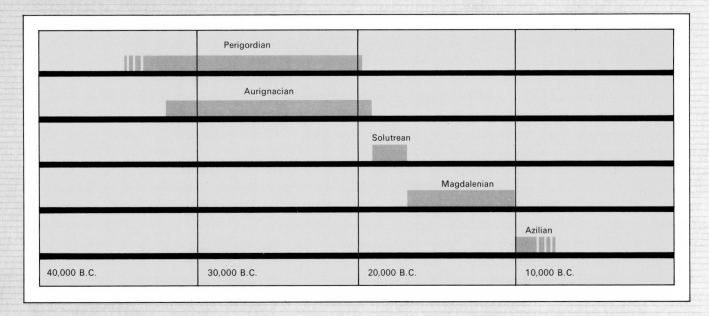

| 40,000 B.C. | 30,000 B.C. | 20,000 B.C. | 10,000 B.C. |

trol uncertain. Where flint was unavailable, men used the most finely textured material they could find, such as quartzite or basalt.

The hard part of knapping is knowing just how and where to apply pressure to the stone. This is done either by striking it directly with a stone, bone or wooden hammer, or indirectly by using a bone punch, or by applying a strong, steady pressure with a pointed tool, such as the tine of an antler. In either case, the force must be controlled with delicate precision, and the knapper must be sensitive to the planes and angles of the stone's structure. Once he gets the knack, he will be able to strike or push off the surface of his stone a flake that is the right size for the tool he wants, with edges that are razor sharp.

These two qualities of certain kinds of stone—a surprising workability in a skilled knapper's hands

and the tendency to break with sharp edges—are the basis of man's early technology, and the capacity to exploit them was for hundreds of thousands of years the measure of his technical progress. In the beginning he employed one of two basic methods: either he knocked two rocks together to sharpen one into a tool like a hand axe or chopper, or he chipped sharp-edged flakes from a stone and used these flakes as his tools. In time he discovered how to strike flakes of consistent size and shape from a piece of stone and how to modify and refine the flakes so that they could be used for specific purposes—a scraper for cleaning hides, a spear point for killing animals, or an axe for chopping or cutting wood.

In Cro-Magnon times an additional refinement was devised. Stoneworkers in Europe learned the knack of striking from a stone core very thin flakes, the so-

called blades which were at least twice as long as they were wide, with double edges so sharp that they sometimes had to be dulled before they could be grasped in the hand. To produce such long, thin blades takes a high degree of skill.

The knapper must first shape a nodule of flint into a roughly cylindrical core and then detach blades, one after another, lengthways from the outside of it by applying strong pressure or a carefully aimed blow to the top edge. The sharp pieces that split off are as long as the core—which might be anywhere from five inches to a foot high—but generally no more than a fraction of an inch thick. Each new blade is struck off right next to the scar left by the first one, and so on around the outside of the core until there is not enough flint left to work with. These blades are then fashioned into tools of many kinds. A good knapper can get more than 50 blades from a single core—and do so in a matter of minutes.

The blade technique has the special advantage of economy over the older flake technique. From a given amount of flint the toolmaker gets more blades from his core, and, in addition, each blade has four to five times as much useful cutting edge as a flake. Such a saving may not have been significant in areas where high-quality flint was plentiful; in England, for example, so-called chalk flint occurs fairly widely in all sizes from egg-sized lumps to 100-pound nodules. But for a band of hunter-gatherers living where good flint was in short supply, the advantages are obvious.

This pierced staff of reindeer antler, found in France's Dordogne region, is a 15,000-year-old example of a puzzling Cro-Magnon artifact that modern experts call a bâton de commandement, on the theory that it symbolized leadership. Later staffs were carved with more ornate decoration.

For the first time, as S. A. Semenov, a Soviet specialist in stone technology, has pointed out, "a person using a small quantity of flint could now achieve a significantly greater result".

Interestingly, blade tools found in the Soviet Union, at Kostenki on the river Don (*pages 51-59*), were fashioned from flint that came from at least 90 miles away. For the hunting people who lived at Kostenki, squeezing out as many blades as possible from a nodule must have been a matter of some importance. The blades themselves were struck at the sources of the flint—representing yet another kind of saving. The nodules could be checked for flaws and imperfect ones discarded; any waste flakes chipped off in the preliminary shaping of the cores could also be left behind at the flint source, lightening the loads of the men who carried the rough blades back to Kostenki.

The blade technique must also have been a boon to hunters going out for several days at a time, with little hope of finding flint or even other fine-grained stones lying about on the ground. They could take a supply of cores or blades with them. They needed spare tools because spear points broke against rocks after inaccurate heaves or were lost in animals that were pierced but got away, and fine-edged knives became chipped cutting through gristle and ligaments. With the blade technique, the hunters could easily replace their losses in the field.

The Cro-Magnons' ever-growing skills as toolmakers seem to have been a critical aspect of their greatly increased cultural diversity. The hand axes of Homo erectus were generally similar whether he lived in Spain or East Africa; likewise, wherever Neanderthal types existed, their scrapers and knives tended to look alike—in some cases so much so that they can seem to have come from the hands of the same toolmaker. But with Cro-Magnon, the picture changes (*chart, page 63*). During the earlier part of his times in western Europe there were, according to the classic French system of classification, two main kinds of tool "industries", called the Aurignacian and the Perigordian after the places where the first examples were found, with several divisions of each. Two other cultures, the Solutrean and the Magdalenian, dominate the latter part of Cro-Magnon times.

The people who produced the Aurignacian and Perigordian scrapers apparently existed side by side or were separated in time by only a brief interlude. This juxtaposition has given rise to puzzling questions. Did each tool industry represent a separate culture? Were the people themselves physically different from one another? Were the various tool kits reflections of variations in the climate and animal and plant life each group encountered? Or were they showing only stylistic differences? Perhaps one population was in some cases producing different tools—or the same tools but in different quantities—to suit seasonal activities and various situations.

It now seems certain that some of the variations in tool manufacture were simply expressions of individuality or of preference by groups of craftsmen, rather than differences in functional needs. Toolmakers dwelling in the same region and possibly related to each other developed a particular way of flintworking that produced tools of similar form. They clung to their style, passing it to new generations as an expression of their identity—a signature. Certainly in his art and decoration and jewellery, Cro-

LAURENT

HEUREUSE PRÉHISTOIRE

PIERRE FANLAC
PÉRIGUEUX

SPOOFING PREHISTORY

Pierre Laurent, a noted French archaeological illustrator, pokes fun at his colleagues in his book Heureuse Préhistoire (above). At right, paired drawings contrast widely accepted explanations for three Cro-Magnon artifacts with Laurent's own facetious views, alleging that the bone staff, considered a symbol of leadership, was in fact a quoit, and that barbed spears and spear throwers were actually used as combs and back-scratchers.

Magnon man was producing clear evidence of a growing expressiveness and self-awareness. Quite possibly some of his tools reflected the same trend.

However individualistic the Cro-Magnon tool industries may have been in style, in utility they had much in common. All produced more specialized tools than earlier men had used. Archaeologists identify 60 or 70 types of tools in the tool kits of some Neanderthals —scrapers meant to be held horizontally, knives with blunted backs, others with double edges and so on. But they count over 100 types in the tool kits of the Cro-Magnons—knives for cutting meat, knives for whittling wood, scrapers for bone, scrapers for skin, perforators for making holes, stone saws, chisels, pounding slabs and countless others. Cro-Magnon man was the great innovator. Among other things, he is believed to have taken to putting bone and antler handles on many of his stone tools, such as axes and knives. The handles increased his application of energy to the tools by as much as two to three times, by providing him with a firmer grasp and enabling him to use to a much greater extent the muscle power of his arm and shoulder.

One of the most important tools that Cro-Magnon man developed was a cutter called a burin. It is tempting to say he invented the burin, but in fact it had existed in a few tool kits of Neanderthal man and even Homo erectus. With the first modern man, however, the burin was gradually improved and became more important and much more numerous. A burin was a kind of chisel; today the name is given to a fine steel-cutting tool used by engravers preparing copper plates. In the Stone Age it was a tool with a strong, sharply bevelled edge or point used to cut, incise and shape other materials, such as bone, antler, wood and sometimes stone. Thus it differed from most other stone tools of prehistory in that it was not used by itself to kill animals, cut meat, clean hides or chop down saplings for tent poles. One of its chief functions was to make other tools and implements—like the machine tools of the modern age. With a tool that made other tools, Cro-Magnon man's technology could expand many times faster than ever before.

The burin probably helped produce many wooden implements, but only fragments of these have survived. So the best record of the object's effectiveness is found in the surviving tools it shaped, superb tools that, like the burin itself, stand out as a mark of Cro-Magnon sophistication.

Three organic raw materials, bone, antler and ivory, helped supply the needs of Cro-Magnon man's ever-expanding economy, and the burin made possible their widespread exploitation. Homo erectus and Neanderthal man had used bone to some extent —for scraping or piercing or digging—but not nearly so much as the Cro-Magnons did. In a typical Neanderthal site perhaps 25 out of a thousand tools turn out to be made of bone; the rest are stone. In some Cro-Magnon encampments the mix may be as much as half and half or even greater.

Bone and antler and ivory were the wonder materials of Cro-Magnon times, much the way plastics are today. Less brittle and therefore more workable, much stronger and more durable than wood, they could be cut, grooved, chiselled, scraped, sharpened, shaped. They could be finely worked into tiny implements like needles, or used for heavy work—a deer antler makes an excellent pick, a mammoth leg bone cracked down its length needs only minor mod-

Text continued on page 70

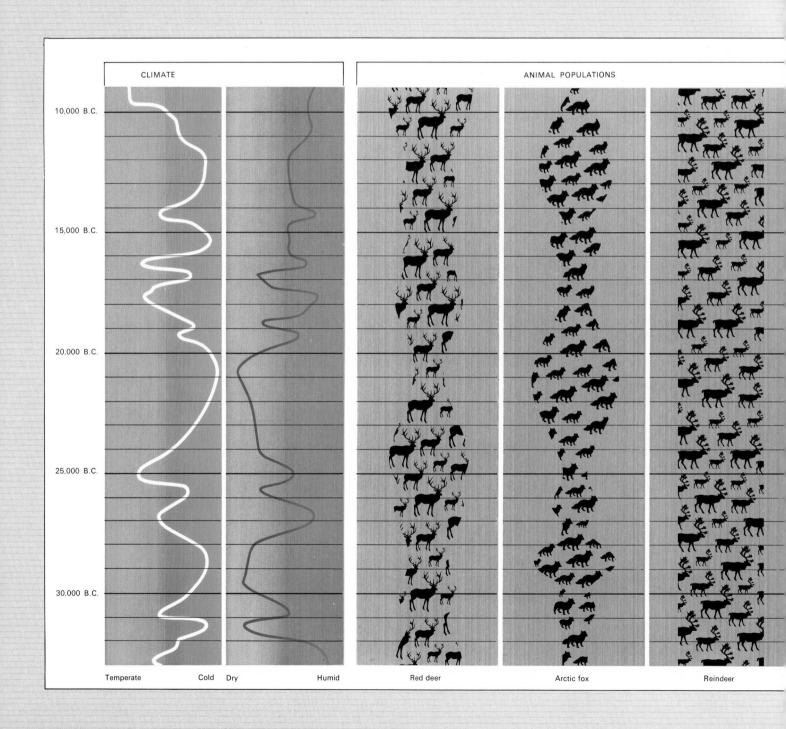

CLIMATE		ANIMAL POPULATIONS		
Temperate Cold	Dry Humid	Red deer	Arctic fox	Reindeer

VEGETATION

eciduous trees   Coniferous trees

Swings of Climate— and a Change in Life Styles

The Cro-Magnons of the Vézère and Dordogne valleys of southwestern France lived through more rapid and extreme fluctuations in their immediate environment than man has since had to endure. As the diagram at left indicates, back-and-forth shifts in climate from mild and humid to cold and dry caused changes in the area's vegetation, and as plant life changed so did animal life. Such frequent oscillations in the environment continually affected man's way of living—his food supply, his need for warm clothing and shelter, and the distances he had to travel to get his food.

The diagram shows how fluctuations in temperature, animal life and vegetation were inter-related during the 24,000-year span from 33,000 B.C. to 9000 B.C. For example, when the climate became milder and damper, as it did in the centuries preceding 25,000 B.C., the red deer population expanded slightly while that of the foxes dwindled—but the reindeer, always able to survive either on lush grass or on low-growing sedges, lichens and mosses, did no worse and no better than they had before. In this period of temperate weather, both deciduous and coniferous trees flourished.

At other times, such as the period before 20,000 B.C., when the temperature dropped sharply and the air became dry, trees dwindled in number and southwestern France's forested terrain turned into open, steppelike grassland. Later on, however, around 15,000 B.C., the climate gradually turned humid while remaining relatively cold, causing the conifers to prosper and cover the landscape with stands of pines and firs.

ifications and a handle to become an efficient shovel. Ivory could be steamed and bent, adding yet another dimension to toolmaking.

Best of all, the very animals that Cro-Magnon men hunted and depended on for food provided these materials in abundance. All animals have bone, of course, and many of the large animals—red deer, reindeer, mammoth—had antlers or tusks as well. Antlers almost seemed to be nature's gift to man because he did not have to kill an animal to obtain them: every year the deer dropped their old ones, which lay on the ground for the picking up. Since reindeer and red deer were at one time or another perhaps the most abundant game animals in western Europe, antler was used there more than bone or ivory. In parts of eastern Europe and Siberia, where wood was relatively scarce, skeletons from giant mammoth that had died a natural death or had been trapped by hunters were a source of tools. One mammoth tusk might measure over nine feet and weigh more than 100 pounds; there were a lot of implements to be made from that much ivory.

The only problem with bone, antler and ivory is that they required a special kind of tool to work them. And that is where the burin came in. With its strong chisel point, the burin could easily scratch or dig into bone without breaking. To cut up a bone, the toolmaker could incise a deep groove around the bone and then, with a sharp blow, break it cleanly at the cut, just as a glazier today cuts a groove in a glass pane before breaking it.

To get slivers for needles, points and awls, it was necessary only to draw a burin repeatedly lengtnways down a bone to score two parallel grooves deep enough to hit the soft centre (*pages 88-89*). Then the

piece of hard material between the grooves was pried out and ground to shape. Other pieces of bone could be turned into spatulas, scrapers, beads, bracelets, digging tools and more.

In addition to domestic utensils, bone and antler provided spear points, lances and barbed harpoon tips, with which Cro-Magnon could take advantage of bountiful supplies of game. Probably at no time since have there been so many edible grazing animals roaming the face of the earth: in Europe and Asia there were mammoth, horses, red deer, pigs, reindeer and bison; in Africa lived all the animals that are known there today, as well as a great many others that are now extinct, including enormous relatives of the buffalo, hartebeest and zebra. For Cro-Magnon man, as British archaeologist Grahame Clark puts it, these animals existed "to convert vegetation into meat and fat and raw materials such as hides, sinews, bones and antlers"—and the first modern men bent their considerable ingenuity to the task of getting full value from nature's bounty.

Two dazzling examples of their hunting success have been turned up by archaeologists in Europe. Near the town of Pavlov, in modern Czechoslovakia, excavations have revealed the remains of over 100 mammoth in one giant bone heap; near Solutré, in France, an even more staggering bone pile contains the fossils of an estimated 10,000 wild horses lying in a tangled heap at the bottom of a high cliff. The mammoth bones are apparently the leavings of hunters who trapped them in pitfalls; the horses had perhaps been stampeded off the cliff over a period of many years, even generations, by intelligent hunters who were familiar down to the last detail with the terrain of the region and the behaviour of their victims.

In fact, it is likely that the people of this period —including the ancestors of the American Indians who would in time be ranging the plains of North America—understood more about hunting large herd animals than any other men in history. They undoubtedly knew just what plants the animals preferred to eat; they knew when seasonal migrations began and how fast the animals travelled; they knew what panicked them and what soothed them. They knew how to drive them into pit traps and how to snare them with baited thong nooses, how to guide them into natural or man-made corrals, either by stampeding them or herding them quietly from a discreet distance. Once trapped, the animals could be dispatched with spears or knives and butchered on the spot. The meat was then taken back to camp, perhaps in some sort of processed form, possibly cut up in strips and smoked or sun-dried.

There can also be little doubt that these hunters knew a great deal about the anatomy of their victims —and the virtue of eating certain of their organs. Today the inland Alaskan Eskimos save the adrenal glands of slaughtered caribou to give to young children and pregnant women. Chemical analysis of the gland revels an astonishingly high content of vitamin C, an essential but otherwise hard-to-come-by element of the Eskimo diet. Without overestimating the Cro-Magnon hunter's knowledge in these matters, it can be assumed that he, too, knew exactly which parts of the animals he hunted were good, and also which parts were good for him.

Cro-Magnon's profound understanding of his prey, combined with significant technical advances in his hunting equipment, paid off in increased food supplies. Men had long had wooden spears with fire-hardened tips or sharp stone heads to thrust or throw at their prey, but the effectiveness of a thrown spear against even a young deer, to say nothing of a thick-skinned giant aurochs, must have been marginal, especially if the animal was in full retreat. The Cro-Magnon hunters made the spear an effective weapon for killing their prey at a greater distance by inventing the spear thrower.

The oldest tangible evidence of this rodlike device comes from the cave of La Placard in France, and dates from about 14,000 years ago. Here several fragments of spear throwers were discovered, including a length of bone with a hooked end that looks like nothing so much as an oversized crochet needle. All told, more than 70 reindeer-antler spear throwers have turned up in southwestern France and near Lake Constance, but there is a curious dearth of them elsewhere in the Old World, perhaps because they were made of perishable wood and rotted away. By about 10,000 years ago, the wooden spear thrower was being used by the Indians of North and South America —the Aztecs called it the atlatl. The Eskimos employed it until recently and Australian aborigines still use it today, and call it a womera.

The spear thrower is, in the simplest terms, an extension of a man's arm. It is a foot to two feet long, with a handle at one end and a point or hook at the other to engage the butt end of the spear (*pages 28-29*). The hunter holds the thrower behind his shoulder, hook up, and lays the spear along it so that the spear points forward and slightly upwards. When throwing, he swings his arm forward and snaps his wrist, launching the spear with great velocity from the end of the thrower at the top of its arc—taking advantage of the centrifugal force thus generated. The

Text continued on page 76

Catching Fish with Stones

If Cro-Magnon man was not the first fisherman, he was the first to make fishing an essential part of his life and to take full advantage of the rich haul of food waiting to be harvested from rivers and sea.

In the Dordogne region of France alone, thick deposits of scales and bones attest to his skill at exploiting this rich resource. Chief among the fish he took here were salmon, which swarmed upstream in large numbers to spawn. How they were caught is not clear from archaeological evidence, but the Dordogne people presumably used tools and techniques that some hunter-gatherers still employ.

In this scene a Cro-Magnon band is shown fishing at a stone weir—similar to those constructed until recently by Canada's Netsilik Eskimos. A narrow opening in the weir funnels the salmon into an enclosure where men and women can easily spear them. The implement they use, the leister, a long pole with three prongs on the end, was also employed by the Netsilik. The central point impales the fish while two pliable barbed tines keep it from wriggling free.

Each fish thus speared is pierced through the gills with a needle-like bone and strung on a sinew rope. The fishermen keep their hands free for this work by using a technique demonstrated by the man in the weir at far right; they carry their needles clenched between their teeth.

Wielding trident-like leisters, Cro-Magnons spear salmon trapped in a stone weir they built across th

...river Dordogne. The man at centre drags a string of fish to the bank where women and children, too old or too young to fish, clean and dry the catch.

At low tide on the South African coast, men, women and children gather a variety of seafood. The man squatting in the foreground baits a fish

Fishing with a Bone Sliver

This scene of fishing and shellfish gathering looks at first glance like any that could be found today around the world's coastlines. But it reconstructs life on the shore at Nelson Bay, South Africa, 12,000 years ago, and differs in at least one basic respect from a modern depiction of fishing: the men casting lines into the sea have no hooks or nets; instead they use an effective device called a fish gorge, a straight bone sharpened at both ends and tied in the middle to a sinew line. Baited, the gorge is tossed into the sea; when a fish bites, the gorge becomes stuck in its throat, and the fisherman pulls in his catch.

The women, following a division of labour still common among many contemporary bands of hunter-gatherers, collect shellfish, filling their sealskin bags with mussels, limpets and abalones. The children, too, make their own contribution of food. In the drawing, the girl in the foreground catches a crab, while the two youths behind her examine a small octopus left stranded in a tidal pool.

gorge with an oyster, while the women near by pry limpets from the rocks with thin bone blades.

hunter holds onto the thrower, which may have a thong tied to its end to go around the wrist. The spear travels faster than if hand-thrown because the extension of the throwing arm provides more leverage; its front end moves faster than the hand holding it.

Modern experiments have demonstrated the great advantage a spear thrower gives. A seven-foot spear can be thrown no more than 60 or 70 yards when launched from a man's hand, but it can be heaved up to 150 yards with a spear thrower, and it can kill a deer at 30 yards. This increase in range gave the ancient hunter a tremendous advantage. No longer did he have to get within a short distance of his prey; moreover, he could get a crack at animals before they spooked and ran away. Now a man could, when the occasion arose, hunt alone instead of in groups, because it was no longer necessary to surround an animal in order to get a spear into it. And, of course, the spear thrower made hunting safer, for hunters did not have to get so close to dangerous teeth, antlers and hoofs. The benefits are obvious: hunters who killed more often and got hurt less lived better—and longer—lives.

The first spear throwers were undoubtedly wood—as the Australian womeras are today—but soon they were also being made from antler. Those late Cro-Magnon people who are known as the Magdalenians embellished many of their throwers with carved figures and designs and may even have painted them—one bears traces of red ochre in its hollows and some have black painted into the eyes. Others display exquisite renderings of animals, including horses, deer, ibexes, bison, birds and fish (*page 102*)—a combination of aesthetics and utility that is echoed in many aspects of Cro-Magnon man's life. At least

The oldest-known firestone, this iron pyrite—shown enlarged one and one half times—is from a Belgian cave where it was left 10,000 or more years ago. The deep groove was worn into the rounded pyrite as it was repeatedly struck with flint to produce sparks. The Cro-Magnons were apparently the first to discover that flint and iron pyrite used in combination yielded sparks hot enough to ignite tinder.

three that are exquisitely carved express a Rabelaisian sense of humour—each shows an ibex defecating.

Other functional advances were in the weapon itself. By this time, the hunters had realized that a barbed point would do more damage than a smooth one. Harpoon-style points, fashioned from bone or antler, often had several barbs on one or both sides. Another development stemmed from the difficulty of killing an animal outright by one spear wound alone; the hunters would have to follow it for a while until loss of blood made the prey weak enough for the men to kill. To speed this process, some hunters developed bone spearheads with grooves along each side—runnels apparently designed to increase the flow of blood from the wound.

Another implement that may have been connected with the hunt is a curious object that has come to be called a *bâton de commandement* (*page 64*), or a staff of authority. Made of antler or bone, *bâtons* vary in length, but are seldom more than a foot long; they are usually Y- or T-shaped, and they always have a hole bored through them at the fork of the Y or near the top of the T. And unlike the clearly deadly spear points and harpoons, they are intriguingly ambiguous in their function.

Many archaeologists think *bâtons* had a primarily ritual function, serving, like sceptres, as symbols of power and status for those entitled to carry them; some are boldly phallic in design. Perhaps they were also considered to have some sort of magical powers. A more prosaic explanation, offered by other archaeologists, is that they were arrow straighteners —if a bent arrow shaft or rod is thrust through the hole and held at both ends, leverage can be applied with the *bâton* to straighten it, especially if the shaft

has been softened by steaming or soaking beforehand. Then again, the *bâtons* may have been used as hunting tools, serving as handles for a kind of leather sling in which the thongs were passed through the hole and tied together. Several other suggestions have been offered to explain the *bâtons*, ranging from the mundane—tent pegs—to the whimsical (*page 67*). And still the mystery remains.

A different kind of puzzle concerns Cro-Magnon's use of the bow and arrow. There is no clear-cut archaeological evidence that he used such a weapon until, at best, the very end of his period of dominance. Since bows are normally made of wood and sinew or gut, it would be a lucky accident indeed if any had survived the last ice age. A couple of bows have been uncovered in Denmark that date back approximately 8,000 years, and a larger number of stone-tipped wooden arrow shafts, perhaps 10,000 years old, have been found in camps of reindeer hunters in northern Germany. In a cave in La Colombière, in France, there have been found small stones, possibly over 20,000 years old, with pictures scratched on them that may represent feathered projectiles; whether they were arrows or dartlike spears, however, is uncertain.

1 is clear, though, that Cro-Magnon man had the wit and ingenuity to invent the bow. He knew that saplings bend under tension and spring back when released; he had leather thongs and almost certainly knew that dried animal gut and sinew made a strong and flexible cord. Believing this, many archaeologists today are convinced that some Cro-Magnon hunters did indeed use the bow before 10,000 B.C., despite the lack of physical proof.

Certainly the bow would have given Cro-Magnon

man an enormous advantage when hunting. The spear thrower, no matter how valuable an aid, required him to break cover and stand out in the open where he could be spotted by his prey; an unsuccessful launch would have scared off the target. But with the bow, he could remain hidden. If he missed with his first arrow, he could shoot again—and again. Moreover, the arrow was swifter than the spear—and its striking power was greater over a longer distance. And it could be shot at running prey, as well as at a variety of animals big and small, including birds on the wing, with a better chance of hitting them.

Perhaps even more significant than the invention of the spear thrower or bow in helping Cro-Magnon man to expand his food supply and make a living in varied environments was his development of fishing gear. Men had earlier availed themselves of the bounty offered by streams, rivers and the sea; but for some Cro-Magnon peoples, fishing became almost a way of life. The record left by the hunter-gatherers who lived in Nelson Bay Cave in South Africa, for example, shows that here again an improved technology was vital to success.

One ingenious development was a device called the leister: a trident-like spear with a point and two curving prongs of bone that held the fish securely after it had been lanced. Another was the fish gorge, a small sliver of bone or wood, perhaps two inches long, with a leather or sinew line tied around its middle. A fisherman dropped his baited line into the water; the gorge, once swallowed by a fish, cocked sideways in its throat so that it could not come out easily; and the fisherman hauled in his catch.

At a slightly later date, in South Africa and perhaps in Europe, men began catching fish in much greater numbers than ever before. Small, grooved, cylindrical stones found in South Africa may have been weights on nets made of thongs or plant fibres. With a net, two or three fishermen could now catch a whole school of fish in one sweep.

The weir, a stone corral for trapping fish still employed by primitive peoples, was probably used also. This would have been especially effective on rivers such as the Dordogne and Vézère in France, where spawning salmon swarmed upstream in great numbers. It seems likely that at the spawning season parties went to the fishing grounds to lay in a supply of salmon for the whole band, which may have had its home base miles away. The fish may have been cleaned and perhaps sun-dried or even smoked at the place where they were caught and then carried to camp. At Solvieux, in France, a large rectangular area carefully paved with small stones has been excavated. Its placement and design strongly hint that it was used as a fish-drying platform.

The systematic exploitation on a worldwide basis of the waters' abundant protein resources—which included great quantities of shellfish as well as fish —was highly significant, points out physical anthropologist Bernard Campbell of UCLA, not only because it broadened the base of the human diet but because it led men towards the next great step in cultural evolution: settled living. With fish and shellfish as a dependable supplement to their regular meat and plant foods, Cro-Magnons did not have to move around so much in quest of sustenance. With nets they could gather more nourishment with less effort than they could as nomadic hunter-gatherers, and thus could support a greater number of people in one

Dating back 12,000 years, this earthenware shard from a cave in southern Japan is believed to be the oldest remnant of pottery. The wavelike decoration was probably formed by affixing clay strips to the vessel just before firing. What the pottery was used for is not known, since this piece and others found near by give no clue to the original shape.

place. In a world with a rapidly expanding population, the approach to a sedentary way of life was a crucial development.

Improving their tools and food-gathering techniques was a major preoccupation of the last ice-age men, but this was not their only concern. As they learned to help themselves more prodigally from nature's bounty, they also found ways to protect themselves more effectively from nature's rigours. The fabrication of carefully sewn, fitted clothing enabled them to conquer the far north and eventually to penetrate the virgin continent of North America.

The hide clothing of these people was probably much like that of the Eskimos of recent times. A tunic or pullover, with tightly sewn seams to keep heat from escaping, pants, easily tucked into boots, and some sort of sock, perhaps of fur, would have been warm enough in all but the coldest weather. For frigid days, outer clothing consisting of a hooded parka, mittens and high boots would have served to keep a person from freezing. Female figurines from Stone Age Russia seem to be clothed in fur. Even in more moderate climates, good sewn clothing was an advantage; the earliest eyed needles to be discovered were fashioned by the same expert Solutrean craftsmen who produced the laurel-leaf blades.

As important as warm, well-fitted clothing for the hunter-gatherers who challenged the glacial climate of the north was fire. From the time of Homo erectus, humans had used fire to cook their food, provide light, keep themselves warm and ward off marauding animals; but the Cro-Magnons added new dimensions to the use of fire by man. For one thing, they were the first to leave proof of their ability to strike a fire quickly whenever they needed one. A cave site in Belgium yielded a beautifully rounded piece of mineral called iron pyrite. This substance is one of the few natural minerals from which flint will strike sparks that will set dry tinder on fire—sparks struck from two flints or two ordinary rocks are not hot enough to do so. What is more, the Belgian pyrite has a groove showing where it had been struck again and again with pieces of flint (*page 76*). Since iron pyrite is not easy to find lying about on the ground, each such fire-stone was undoubtedly a cherished item that would have been carried wherever a band roamed.

A more dramatic example of Cro-Magnon man's growing mastery of fire—evidence of which has turned up in sites in the Soviet Union and France —seems very prosaic at first glance: a series of shallow grooves dug into the bottom of a hearth and a tail-shaped channel curving away from it. So simple an innovation may well have been overlooked many times in earlier archaeological excavations. But, in fact, it was the first small step towards the blast furnaces of modern steel mills. The point is that fires burn hotter if they get more air—that is, more oxygen. The grooves and channels in those prehistoric fireplaces allowed more air to reach the fuel, and the fires in them could thus burn hotter.

The ancient Russians who built these special hearths needed them because of the fuel they used. In an area where wood was scarce, they had to turn to a kind of fuel that normally did not burn well. The new source of supply was the same wonder material that revolutionized toolmaking—bone. Although it is hard to ignite and burns inefficiently, since only about 25 per cent of it is combustible material, bone gives off adequate heat. That the Russians did burn it is proved by the lack of charred wood and the consid-

A 27,000-year-old fingerprint (or toe print) shows up on this discarded lump of clay, fire-hardened into ceramic about 15,000 years before the first known pottery vessels were made. The shapeless lump, found beside a kilnlike pit at Dolni Vestonice in Czechoslovakia, was apparently fired by accident, along with many animal figures found in fragments near by.

erable quantities of bone ash found in their specially vented hearths.

The hearth was home, and Cro-Magnon man, who changed so much else, also changed the concept of home. Where he lived in caves and rock shelters that had protected his predecessors, he seems, in some places at least, to have kept cleaner house than those earlier tenants had—litter was thrown outside instead of being allowed to pile up inside.

It was in regions that offered no ready-made habitations that Cro-Magnon man's home improvements were most noticeable. Particularly in central and eastern Europe and Siberia, remnants of many sturdy domiciles have been found in open country. They apparently were occupied on a semipermanent basis. One of the best-known sites is Dolni Vestonice, in south central Czechoslovakia, and from the buried remains of this ancient community an intriguing picture of man's domestic life in Europe 27,000 years ago can be reconstructed:

On a grass-covered slope dotted with a few isolated trees, a settlement of five huts was partially surrounded by a simple wall of mammoth tusks and bones stuck into the ground and piled about with brush and turf. One hut was set 90 yards apart from the others. The four close together were supported by wooden posts leaning slightly towards the middle, like tent poles, and planted in the earth with rocks piled around their bases for support. The walls were animal skins, presumably dressed and sewn together, then drawn over the posts and anchored to the ground with stones and heavy bones.

A small stream meandered down the slope close by the houses, and the ground all around had been hard-packed by the feet of the generations of people who lived here. In an open place among the huts there was a large fire; very likely a fire-tender kept it going by throwing on chunks of bone. Apparently it burned all the time to keep prowling animals away.

Inside the largest hut, about 50 feet long by 20 feet wide, were five shallow hearths dug in the floor. One was equipped with two long mammoth bones stuck in the ground to support a roasting spit. In these relatively comfortable surroundings it is easy to imagine a man sitting on a boulder making tools—working with the purposeful, deceptively slow movements of a master craftsman, using a bone hammer to strike delicate blades from a cylindrical chunk of flint, the core. Meanwhile, from a far end of the hut might have come a clear, high-pitched sound like a bird's call. Its source would have been a woman blowing into the end of a piece of hollow bone that had two or three holes pierced in its length—what humans some 25,000 years later would call a penny whistle has been found at Dolni Vestonice.

But the most startling discovery at this Czech site is the remains of the small hut up the slope that was set apart from the others. The hut had been cut into the hill, which formed its back wall; its sides consisted partly of a low wall of stones and clay, and the entrance faced downhill.

Inside a visitor would have seen a hearth quite different from those apparent in the other huts; this one had an earthen dome on top of fiercely glowing coals. It was an oven for baking clay, a kiln—one of the very first ever built. Even at this early date the raw material that was baked in the kiln was a specially prepared substance. No simple mud from a stream bank, it was earth mixed with powdered bone to make the heat spread evenly as the oven baked, or fired, the clay into a new, rock-hard material. This is the first example in technological history of what was to become a ubiquitous process—the combination and treatment of two or more dissimilar substances to make a useful product unlike either starting substance—eventually leading to glass, bronze, steel, nylon and most of the other materials of everyday life. It would be another 15,000 years or so before other men, living in what is now Japan, learned to turn clay into pots; yet, as the evidence from Dolni Vestonice attests, ceramics had already been invented.

When the kiln hut was first investigated in 1951, its sooty floor was littered with fragments of ceramic figurines. There were animal heads—bears, foxes, lions. In one particularly beautiful lion head there is a hole simulating a wound, perhaps intended to help some hunter inflict a similar wound on a real lion. The floor was also cluttered with hundreds of clay pellets bearing the fingerprints of the prehistoric artisan (*page 80*); he probably pinched them off his lump of unbaked clay when he first began to knead and shape it to his desire. And there were limbs broken from little animal and human figures. They may have cracked off in the baking, or when the ancient ceramist tossed aside a work that failed to please him.

But more intriguing than any waste fragments or even clay animal figures on the hut floor are the human statuettes found there—particularly the female figures. Unlike the animals, they are not naturalistic but almost surreal. They have bulging breasts and buttocks, distorted arms and legs that taper to points. Experts today still wonder about these so-called Venuses (*pages 92, 98-100*). Were they household goddesses whose pointed legs were stuck in the ground to hold them upright as they watched over hearth and home? Were they fertility symbols whose ample figures were supposed to enhance fecundity? Certainly they are beautiful objects in spite of their grotesque proportions. They have a grace and dignity, a stylized plasticity, that make them comparable to some modern sculpture.

And the man who made them—was he simply a craftsman? Was he an artist? A shaman, a man of magic? The only certain thing is that art and industry were now firmly fused. It was one of Cro-Magnon man's lustrous achievements.

Toolmaking: A Modern Master Demonstrates the Ancient Art

Jacques Tixier, a maker of stone tools, carefully inspects the flint nodule he will use.

Cro-Magnon tools, no matter how simple they might appear at first glance, actually required expert planning and craftsmanship to execute. Indeed, the men who made them were such masters that only a few patient present-day experimenters have been able to duplicate their efforts.

One of the most capable and versatile of the contemporary toolmakers —a man whose skills would have enabled him to survive in Cro-Magnon times—is a native of Bordeaux, Professor Jacques Tixier, shown at left with a nodule of raw flint and some of the stone and antler implements he uses in his work.

Now head of the laboratory of lithic —or stone—studies at the *Institut de Paléontologie Humaine* in Paris, Tixier first became interested in stone tools as a teacher and later as a doctoral student. Soon he tried making his own and, after a few fumbling efforts, got the knack. In time, he taught himself the most characteristic—and most difficult—of the European Cro-Magnon stoneworking methods, the so-called blade technique.

In the series of photographs beginning on the following page, Professor Tixier demonstrates the blade technique, makes tools from the pieces of flint thus obtained, and uses some of them to shape another basic Cro-Magnon raw material, antler, into a sewing needle and the ubiquitous, but puzzling, *bâton de commandement*.

The First Step: A Basic Blade

Before he could make blade tools, the Cro-Magnon stoneworker had to find a good flint nodule. A cracked or fissured one would not do, nor one that produced a dull sound when it was tapped, indicating flaws. On occasion, to improve its texture, the toolmaker apparently heated up the flint; this made its crystalline structure more compact once it had cooled.

After settling on just the right nodule, the stoneworker chipped it into a roughly cylindrical shape or core. This was the first step in the actual toolmaking process, and the most important one. A poorly prepared core did not yield long, thin, sharp blades like the one shown at far right, actual size —the kind the stoneworker needed for making fine tools.

Making blades

1. *To prepare the nodule for the making of blades, Tixier strikes it repeatedly with a stone hammer until chips break off—one is seen sliding from the piece of soft leather covering Tixier's leg.*

2. *Having switched to a hammer made of elk antler in order to apply less force to the flint and knock off smaller pieces, Tixier sends chips flying through the air. They are seen next to Tixier's knee.*

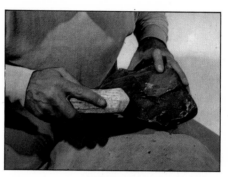

5. *Taking up his antler hammer once again, Tixier goes back to work; he refines the ridge to make it straight and regular enough so that the first blade will split from the core in one long and thin piece.*

6. *Tixier holds up the stone to show the straightened ridge. This completes the first step in the making of blades—the most critical part of the work, since a badly prepared core will not yield usable blades.*

9. *Tixier has just detached the first blade and holds it in his hand. The blade has left two new ridges. By placing the punch behind the top of each ridge and hitting it, Tixier will detach two new blades.*

10. *After many blades have been removed, the core takes on a grooved appearance. Several ridges are visible, and Tixier has placed his punch at the top of one of them, ready to remove still another blade.*

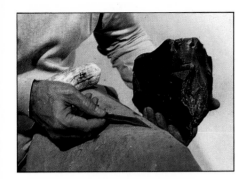

3. *After removing numerous chips from the nodule, Tixier holds one in his right hand. This is the usual size of chips knocked off by the antler hammer; a hammerstone produces larger ones.*

4. *Tixier studies the ridge he has made by chipping pieces from both sides of the core. To obtain his first blade, he will knock off the entire ridge—but the ridge is too wavy to yield a good blade.*

7. *Ready to strike off the first blade, Tixier holds the core down firmly with his foot; to keep it from jiggling he has put a piece of antler under it. He then places an antler punch or rod just behind the ridge.*

8. *This picture, which was taken from another angle, shows Tixier in the same position, preparing to hit the punch with his antler hammer. The punch enables him to direct the effect of the blow.*

11. *Tixier shows how a blade fits back onto the core. But the ridge in the centre of the blade is wavy, and the blade itself is thick and irregular. Ideally, blades should be straight-edged—and quite thin.*

12. *In 30 minutes Tixier has removed 16 blades, shown lying next to the core. Although they are sharp and strong, these blades are not ready for use but must be fashioned into special tools (overleaf).*

Processing Blades into Varied Tools

The blade technique had certain advantages that Cro-Magnons in Europe were quick to exploit. From an economical point of view, it represented a highly efficient use of the raw material, yielding more blades than the older method of chipping tools from a core, and providing from four to five times as much cutting edge. From the blades, the Cro-Magnons made a wide variety of tools.

On the right, Tixier shows how an ancient toolmaker fashioned three basic instruments—a scraper, a perforator and a knife—and also how he used them. Tixier's tools are reproduced at far right in their actual sizes.

Making and using a scraper

1. *About to make a scraper, Tixier holds up the blade on which he will work. It is so thin around the edges that light shines through. The other tools shown on this page were made from similar blades.*

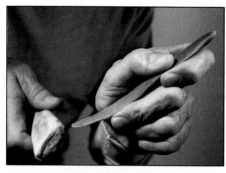

2. *With an antler hammer, Tixier chips off the fragile end of the blade to provide a stubbier, thicker end that will be strong enough to withstand pressure applied to it during the skin-scraping process.*

Making and using a perforator

1. *To make a perforator, an implement that Cro-Magnons used as a kind of awl or drill, Tixier rests a new blade on a stone anvil, and with the blunt tip of an antler hammer chips a roughly triangular point.*

2. *Tixier now narrows and sharpens the point by pressing it against the edge of a stone to remove small chips. This technique, called pressure flaking, gives Tixier delicate control of the material.*

Making and using a knife

1. *To make a backed knife, that is, a knife with one dull edge, Tixier chips the edge he wants blunted. Since blades have two sharp cutting edges, it is essential to dull one if the knife is to be hand-held.*

2. *Holding the blade in his hand, Tixier now taps it lightly with the antler hammer. This gives him more control, as well as allowing him to dull the sharp ridges still left, and make an even, noncutting edge.*

3. Tixier uses the scraper he has just made to remove the interior membrane from a rabbitskin. Cro-Magnons did this to prevent skins from spoiling, then dried them and used them for warm clothing.

3. With the perforator he has just made, Tixier punches a hole in a piece of leather. Through this hole, Cro-Magnons could pass a sinew. They also used perforators to drill holes in wood, bone or antler.

3. Tixier holds the knife between his thumb and forefinger, pressing the latter against the dull edge, and cuts a strip of meat from a haunch of venison. Such knives work as well as any of steel.

Scraper

Perforator

Knife

Using a Burin to Shape a Needle

One of the most valuable stone tools Cro-Magnon possessed was the burin, a flat, narrow implement with a sharp, strong corner for chiselling and engraving (*far right*). It enabled him to fully exploit bone, antler and ivory, materials that had always been abundant but little used by earlier men. With the burin, he chiselled these materials into a wide range of new tools and other objects—everything from sewing needles, harpoons and spear throwers to bracelets and beads.

In the photographs on the right, Tixier deftly turns a blade into a burin, and then carves out a needle from a portion of antler that he soaked in water beforehand to soften it.

Making a burin

1. *Tixier holds up the blade that he will fashion into a burin—by knocking off one sharp edge to get a thicker edge. But first he must prepare the top end of the blade, which he will strike with a hammer.*

2. *Resting the blade on a stone anvil, with his hammer Tixier shapes the end of the blade to make it thicker and also to accentuate the acute angle of the corner before knocking off the chip.*

Fashioning a needle out of antler

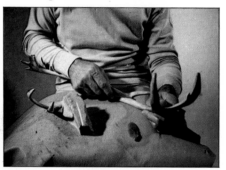

1. *Preparing to make a needle, Tixier now holds the antler in his hands; on his lap are a burin and a piece of grooved sandstone. The groove, which is used to sharpen the needle, was cut with a burin.*

2. *Having scratched the outline of a triangle on the antler, Tixier cuts the first of three grooves. The burin he uses, also made from a blade, was chipped on both sides to give it a finer point.*

5. *Tixier now rubs the wide end of the triangle against a piece of sandstone in order to thin it down. When it is sufficiently thin, he will be able to pierce this end—and make the needle's eye.*

6. *Preparing to make the eye, Tixier holds the triangle in his hand and gently begins to bore a hole with a perforator. He will turn the triangle over and work on the other side to refine the eye.*

3. Having shaped the corner, Tixier holds the hammer perpendicular to the end of the blade and gives one strong blow. This will remove the chip, called the burin spall, and give him a usable burin.

4. The burin spall, or chip, has been removed, and Tixier shows where it came from. Its removal has left a sharp, strong corner, the working part of the burin, with which he can cut into antler.

3. Tixier now finishes carving the triangle. He must cut deep enough to completely separate it from the rest of the antler. If he does not do this, the triangle will splinter when he tries to remove it.

4. By simply pressing his finger on one end, Tixier lifts out the triangle from the cavity. If, in prying it loose, any part of it had remained attached to the antler, the triangle would have broken into pieces.

7. The eye—only one sixteenth of an inch in diameter—is finished, and Tixier uses the burin he was shown making in the first four pictures at top to shape the triangle into a rounded needle.

8. To finish the needle, Tixier sharpens the point by rubbing it back and forth in a groove in a piece of sandstone. The finished needle is pointed enough to penetrate leather or skins easily.

Burin

Needle

The Mystery Tool: A Baton of Antler

One of the most mysterious objects produced by Cro-Magnon toolmakers is the *bâton de commandement*, a sceptre-like rod made of antler, with a hole at one end. Although its function is unknown, the *bâton* itself can be easily duplicated, and here Tixier makes one from the caribou antler he is shown examining in the large photograph at right.

Many of the *bâtons* that have been found in Cro-Magnon sites are ornately carved and are believed to have been used in ceremonies, perhaps to symbolize authority or leadership. But the one that Tixier made—at far right—was deliberately left unornamented to show how it would have looked fresh from the hands of a master Cro-Magnon toolmaker.

Making a bâton de commandement

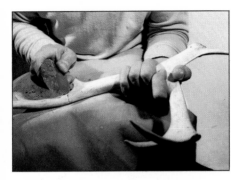

1. *Picking up one of the waste chips he originally knocked off the flint nodule, Tixier uses its strong, sharp edge to deeply score one branch of the antler, which has been softened by soaking.*

2. *Tixier breaks off the branch. He will repeat the process of scoring and breaking in four different places on the piece until he gets the basic, rodlike shape of a Cro-Magnon bâton de commandement.*

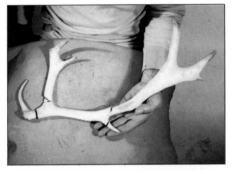

3. *To show the portion of antler used for the bâton, Tixier replaces the four parts he has broken off. In order to finish the bâton, Tixier has only to bore a hole through one of the branched ends.*

4. *With a large perforator, fashioned from another of the waste chips knocked off the nodule, Tixier begins to drill a hole. The hole is always made in the same place, between two of the tines.*

5. *To complete the hole, Tixier bores from the other side. Unlike bone, the antler is as hard in the middle as it is on the outside. Tixier wraps the perforator in a piece of leather to protect his hand.*

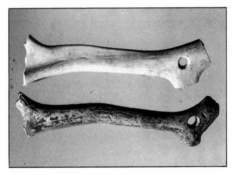

6. *Tixier's bâton at the top lies next to a Cro-Magnon bâton found in France and made about 12,000 years ago. The ancient bâton has a female figure carved on it—but otherwise looks the same as the new one.*

Chapter Four: The Birth of Fine Art

The Venus of Laussel, carved 22,000 years ago in a block of limestone, represents a type of voluptuous female often portrayed by artists of the Cro-Magnon period, perhaps as a fertility symbol. In her right hand she holds an animal horn, suggesting some sort of ritual. The figure was found in 1911 in a cave in France's Dordogne region; it still bears traces of pigment that once coloured it.

Any report on the great age of prehistoric art must pay a few words of tribute to the idle curiosity of dogs and children. These casual explorers sometimes play a crucial rôle, perhaps best exemplified by the discovery of the cave paintings at Altamira, Spain. This find, uncovered by the most haphazard blind luck, opened eyes to the remarkable artistry and skill of the people of Cro-Magnon times.

The tale begins in 1868, when a hunter's dog chased a fox across hilly countryside about 15 miles inland from the port of Santander on the Atlantic coast of Spain. The dog fell among some boulders. When the hunter rescued his pet by pushing aside some fallen rocks, he saw that they had covered the opening of an ancient cave.

This trivial incident set in motion a long, momentous chain of events. The cave, as it happened, was on the summer estate of a Spanish nobleman and amateur archaeologist, Don Marcelino de Sautuola. For seven years no one bothered to tell the Don about the cave—the area is riddled with them. When he finally did look around the vestibule of this cavern, he picked up a number of bones of such ancient animals as bison, megaceros (a huge extinct deer) and primitive horses, but even they were not remarkably rare. It was not until 1878, when he visited the Paris International Exhibition and studied the display cabinets filled with ice-age tools and bone engravings, that he realized he might have a similar treasure on his own property. Then the Don acted wisely. He enlisted a noted French archaeologist, Edouard Piette, to brief him on the ice age—its cultural stages, its stone tools and its engravings of animals.

Now, with an idea of what to look for, Don Marcelino hurried back to Spain, reopened his cave and began to dig into its floor. Compared with other such prehistoric caves, Altamira is medium-sized, extending all told about 900 feet. Beyond a tiny cramped entrance hall, it widens into a zigzag string of three galleries with several lateral extensions, then tapers into a very narrow twisting corridor about 155 feet long. The Don, working on his hands and knees, unearthed near the entrance a number of stone tools. But for these initial researches, the Don's head was bent in the wrong direction.

This error was rectified by the child in the story. One day in 1879 the Don's daughter Maria, aged 12, accompanied her father to the cave and wandered into a chamber, about 85 feet from the entrance, that was little more than a tunnel, between four and a half and five feet from floor to ceiling. Her father had already crawled into this area digging for tools, but Maria was small enough to look around. In the dim light of her lantern, she saw a herd of red animals spread across the ceiling, like the fairy-tale cow that jumped over the moon. Running back to her father, she shouted of her discovery.

The Don stooped to enter the chamber and then gaped upwards to behold a throng of some 25 painted animals, mostly bison. Had he been calm enough to count carefully, he would have spotted, in addition, two horses, a wolf, three female deer and three wild boars. Some were life-sized, or even larger, and in the wavering lamplight they seemed to pulse with life. Coloured in rich browns, reds, yellows and black, they sometimes conformed to the shape of the rock itself; the artist had purposely positioned them to take advantage of the Altamira ceiling's undulating contours. A rounded haunch, for example, was painted over a protuberance in the stone, thus creating a three-dimensional effect that was uncannily realistic.

Don Marcelino was stunned. True, a few animal pictures engraved without colour had been discovered before in a French cave, but here were the first Stone Age paintings that he or any other modern investigator had yet seen. And as the Don blinked at the teeming ceiling, his sense of peering into the remote past might be compared with the feelings of Galileo first peering through his home-made telescope into remote space and seeing the moons on Jupiter. The two events were superficially quite dissimilar; one dealt with the immensity of space, the other with the immensity of time. But in both cases, man was vastly extending the frontiers of his knowledge.

Don Marcelino rushed to Madrid to seek the counsel of his friend, Juan Vilanova y Piera, a professor of palaeontology at the university who had previously advised the noble archaeologist. Vilanova, excited by the news, immediately went to inspect the new discovery. Since he saw no evidence whatsoever that the cavern had been entered since the late ice age, it seemed certain that the pictures could not have been done later. The Don described the discovery in a pamphlet he published. Little Maria had her picture in the newspaper. Among the sightseers who found the road to the cave was the King of Spain, Alfonzo XII, ducking his royal head to enter the bison gallery. (The floor, incidentally, has since been deepened so today's tourists can stand up straight.)

The cave extends under an old farm appropriately called Altamira (high lookout), its entrance opening on a gentle slope in a high tract of meadowland. The immediate landscape is homelike and intimate. But to the south, the majestic Cordillera Cantabrica jabs upwards at the sky, and to the west the Picos de Europa, rising to more than 8,000 feet, are snow-clad most of the year. Nobody knows whether Altamira, at any time in its ancient history, was ever considered a holy place. But its handsome setting suggests the possibility.

The Altamira discovery did not at first impress the academic establishment. Scholars who were prepared to accept the antiquity of man were not prepared to credit him with artistic ability. When in 1880 Vilanova supported Don Marcelino's find before a congress of experts at Lisbon, he was snubbed on an international scale by scholars from Germany, France, Sweden, Norway and England. The consensus was that the art could not possibly be more than 20 years old. A Spanish artist pontificated that the paintings have "none of the character of either Stone Age, archaic, Assyrian or Phoenician art. They are simply the expression of a mediocre student of the modern school." And the nastiest cut of all came from a French expert who pointed out that Don Marcelino had for some years housed a clever artist on his estate, referring to a protégé of the Don's who even then was preparing copies of the cave art. Here was the culprit, the professor hinted, who had sneaked into the ancient cave, equipped with lamps and paints, to create the bogus pictures. The assembled pundits almost gleefully embraced this silly tale, and the Don gave up trying to prove the reality of ice-age art. He had the cave locked, and died in 1888.

The contumely heaped on Don Marcelino was inexcusable, but it must be admitted that his critics had some reason to be sceptical. To them, it seemed incredible that colours, allegedly applied in the ice age, could have stayed so bright, and that the walls of limestone, a substance known to crumble easily, were still intact beneath the pigments. Even more unbelievable, the paintings were done with a controlled grace and style totally at odds with the 19th Century image of primitive men and their barbaric way of life. What the scientists failed to see was the basic similarity in subject and spirit between the Altamira murals and the small animal figures engraved on bone that had already been accepted as belonging to the remote ice age. A study of these small figures by the French palaeontologist Edouard Lartet and the English archaeologist Henry Christy had just been circulated, so it is surprising that knowledgeable scholars would reject almost the same figures in enlarged versions. What would be the most famous of all painted caves had to wait 20 years to be rediscovered and for the Don's faith in it to be justified.

When the antiquity of cave paintings was finally accepted, Cro-Magnon man was firmly established as the first artist. His engravings and paintings were not simply utilitarian objects that happened to be pleasing to look at. They were meant to be looked at, if only by their creators, and they were created to fulfill some inner need. But Cro-Magnon man did not invent art full-blown from nothing. The origins of his artistic impulses were certainly older than he.

For a million years at least, early man left almost no record of art or of an artistic sense. But shiny quartz crystal, found in the Choukoutien caves of China, suggests that even Homo erectus 500,000 years ago may have kept such objects as things of beauty with beneficial properties. And it is not implausible that other early men adorned themselves with feathers, antlers and fur, and performed rhythmic motions and chants for a mixture of reasons that included aesthetic gratification. By Neanderthal times there is clear evidence that stone weapons were being deliberately shaped with eye-pleasing symmetry. So it is logical to suppose that when Cro-Magnon man began to create his graphic record of his own times he had some background in artistic expression and some intuitive grasp of its rules and limits.

Cro-Magnon art falls into two major categories. The first is usually referred to by the French term *art mobilier*, portable art. The second is called parietal art, an Anglicization of the French *art pariétal*, art attached to any permanent surface, such as a cave wall.

The oldest evidence of man's artistic skill is in the first category—little objects of carved bone, antler, ivory or modelled clay that date back at least 30,000 years and that were among man's first valued possessions. His fingers had been to school for aeons, learning how to grip or curl around a rock or bone and how to manipulate a cutting tool. So he progressed naturally to making small decorative articles. He produced these by the countless thousands, perhaps during winter, when his hunting activities were curtailed and he found himself with leisure time. These objects have turned up, whole or fragmented, all the way from France to Siberia, and what they have in common is not only their small size but their attention to detail. Some are even polished and engraved, like the scrimshaw carvings of 19th Century Yankee whalers. They were preserved because they were lost or discarded and became buried in layers of earth or stone in caves, rock shelters and open-air sites where Cro-Magnons camped. A few in Czechoslovakia and the Soviet Union have been discovered hidden in pits close to hearths, suggesting that they were invested with special meaning by their owners.

These little objects bring us closer to Cro-Magnon man because they are part of his everyday life—an adornment of it. Human hands like our own fondled them, used them, hid them, maybe stole them, swapped them or gave them as tribute gifts. The flamboyant cave paintings have stolen the show, but the less pretentious—more human—*art mobilier* holds its own as a special treasure. Its carved animals—antelope, bison, horse, lion, bear—are brimming with life, as if early man was celebrating his new-found capacities for creation, and its decorations go beyond even nature in their lively diversity.

Perhaps most striking of the portable art objects are the representations of humans. Some—notably the disproportionately fat Venus figurines of Europe (*pages 98-99*)—distort the figure with a freedom and confidence that would not be seen again in the West until the 20th Century.

The tendency towards bold patterns is embodied in a unique piece of *art mobilier*, a female image from Predmost, Czechoslovakia, engraved on a mammoth tusk (*page 96*). Here is no bulbous exaggeration of womanly amplitude, but a fantastic idealized figure with a horned, triangular head; ovoid breasts that flank her head; a round target for a belly with a bull's-eye navel; and a wide pelvis—bigger than any other element in the engraving—enclosed in seven ovals. The legs—cut off at the knees—are minimal.

Viewed in its entirety, the Predmost design looks like both a female figure and a huge bizarre mask,

Three decorated objects—two tapering bone rods from France and a mammoth tusk from Czechoslovakia—are thought to have been used in some kind of rites. In the tusk, incised concentric ovals form an abstract version of a woman, hinting that the rods' geometric patterns may also be symbols.

with the breasts representing eyes and the pelvis a gaping mouth. It is possible that the ambiguity of the image was intentional, meant to increase its potency in some sort of magic. Altogether, this geometric work gives an impression of modern sophistication, as if it had been created by Picasso or Miró.

Such linear patterns are often seen in early stages of ancient Egyptian and Greek art. Yet this fantastic engraved Venus was contemporaneous with the realistic little sculptured heads of bears, lions and rhinoceroses found in the same region. So it appears that these versatile Eastern European artists were perfectly capable of producing naturalistic art when they felt the occasion demanded it.

Some naturalistic art appears to be documentary, commemorating human experience. Little flat bone discs from France, each pierced with a hole like a miniature phonograph record, are engraved in various ways. One shows a gentle-faced prehistoric cow. Another is partly naturalistic, for though the man's genitals are clearly human, his head—as so often happens in prehistoric pictures—suggests the head of an animal. On a third (*page 104*), carved from a shoulder bone, a hind is being speared on one face of the disc, while on the opposite side the hind is crumpled on the ground, already struck down. The two pictures combined in this little sequence appear to tell a story, a technique that was to be developed many thousands of years later into religious narrative paintings, cartoon strips and motion-picture films.

Such small, beautiful objects surely became prized keepsakes or sacred relics, bequeathed by one person to another and imbued with sentiment. People became identified by what they used, what they valued, what they wore. Cro-Magnons put on necklaces of fish vertebrae and pierced teeth, affected ivory bracelets, and wore clothes decorated with rows of coloured beads. Personal adornment, in the words of anthropologist John E. Pfeiffer, "involved a new level of assertiveness, a new degree of individuality".

And yet much of *art mobilier* seems to be more than pretties for a Cro-Magnon lady's bosom or *objets d'art* for her fireplace, and may in fact have been associated with religious rites or other esoteric concerns (*Chapter 5*). Though most experts now reject an art-for-art's-sake theory, they concede that a fair amount of work may have been done for the sheer pleasure of it. Each piece of *art mobilier* presented a special challenge. The artist had to figure out how to manipulate the raw material—bone, horn or stone —to best exploit its natural shape and texture. Take, for example, a difficult shape like reindeer antlers. How could the artist transform these jagged, many-branched objects into a sculptured animal or a useful tool? Working out such a problem requires great skill and ingenuity, and ancient artists must have delighted in tackling the puzzle and solving it.

The Romantic poet William Wordsworth had something to say about this kind of enjoyment in his sonnet on the problem of sonnet-writing, with all its strict rules about length and meter: *twas pastime to be bound/Within the Sonnet's scanty plot of ground.* By the same token, the Cro-Magnons must have regarded as something close to "pastime" their formidable task: to be bound within the scanty limits of an antler, a mammoth's tusk or a rock, and yet to utilize these very limitations to create an admirable new object. It has always been an impetus to art to have to meet special demands, provided, of course, that the artist accepts and understands the demands.

This Czech clay figure shows the Venuses' typical traits: huge breasts and belly, shapeless arms, and legs that, though now broken, probably had no feet.

Carved in stone, the Willendorf Venus was found in Austria. Her arms are mere bands resting on her breasts, her hair a woolly helmet over her head and face.

The Riddle of the Misshapen Venuses

Among the most intriguing relics of Cro-Magnon handiwork are the statuettes archaeologists call Venus figurines because of their curvaceous depiction of the female body. Some 60 have been found scattered from France to Siberia—yet all, like the five shown here, were made 20,000 to 27,000 years ago, and most display the same motherly figure. The significance of the Venuses is disputed, but most experts think they are fertility symbols, images of a mother-goddess revered by the Cro-Magnons as the source and protector of all things good. She was the bearer of children, keeper of the home, guardian of the hunt—and may even have been considered the ancestor of the human race.

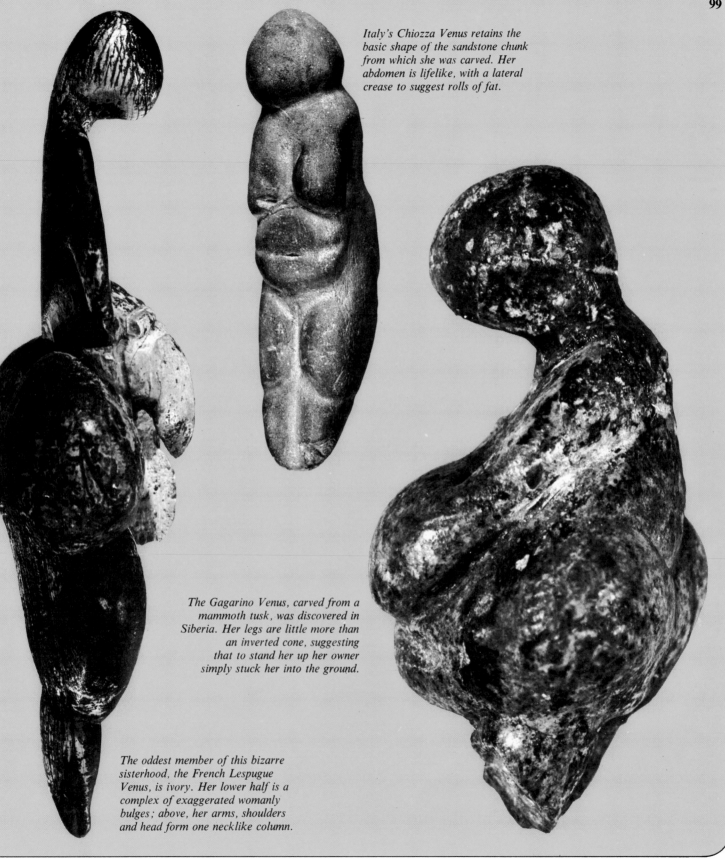

Italy's Chiozza Venus retains the basic shape of the sandstone chunk from which she was carved. Her abdomen is lifelike, with a lateral crease to suggest rolls of fat.

The Gagarino Venus, carved from a mammoth tusk, was discovered in Siberia. Her legs are little more than an inverted cone, suggesting that to stand her up her owner simply stuck her into the ground.

The oddest member of this bizarre sisterhood, the French Lespugue Venus, is ivory. Her lower half is a complex of exaggerated womanly bulges; above, her arms, shoulders and head form one necklike column.

Ingenuity in fitting a design to scanty ground is strikingly demonstrated in an elegant perforated staff that has been identified with equal certainty by opposing experts as one of those mysterious objects, a *bâton de commandement*, and also as a spear thrower (*page 102*). Utilizing the natural curve of a reindeer antler, the staff terminates in the figure of a leaping horse whoosing upwards. Streamlined for flight, the head might be the nose of a rocket, the front legs landing gear retracted under the belly, while the hind legs seem still imprisoned in the staff itself. The horse appears to be springing from some primordial substance, still in the process of creation. But the artist's greatest achievement is that the horse is no mere ornament or excrescence on the baton or spear thrower. It is an organic part of the implement, wholly essential to its usefulness and in harmony with its form. The artist felt strongly that this was how it must be, and he consummated his feeling fully.

Many more examples of such artistic ingenuity can be cited—two headless ibexes hugging or fighting each other on the end of a spear thrower, a scene of reindeer and leaping salmon on an antler, a crouching hyena getting ready to spring. But the special genius of this art is perhaps best summed up in the controversial figure of a bison that is licking its own back (*page 104*).

Some experts say this little figure, carved from a reindeer antler, was once part of a spear thrower.

Two slender ivory figurines from France and Siberia suggest that Cro-Magnons admired other forms of femininity besides the squat Venuses shown on pages 98-99. Yet these too are distorted: the headless figure was apparently made that way, though its legs were carved with respect for anatomical detail; the other has abnormally long legs.

Others disagree, saying its use is unclear. But what matters is the artist's success in catching a precise instant in time when a bison turned his head to pull its tongue across its flank, and in sending this peaceful image to us across some 15,000 years. The image bounced, so to speak, from the bison to the artist's eye and mind, then onto the bone he was carving, finally into the pages of this book, and at last lodges in the eye and brain of the reader. The artist took pains that the image should be clearly visible. And modern eyes record his data. Coarse hair on bulging brow. Muzzle fringed with soft fur. Almond-shaped eye, heavily rimmed. Nostrils also rimmed. Left horn sunken. Right horn in low relief. Small ear. Dewlap and mane long and wavy. Across the awesome millennia a simple act of flesh and blood is transmitted: bison licking an itch.

The peculiar charm of this work lies in the originality of the animal's pose, with its head doubled back against the body, thus utilizing the shape of antler bone in a delightfully ingenious way. But even on this point the experts disagree completely. André Leroi-Gourhan recognizes the ingenuity, saying "the pose is dictated by the shape of the reindeer antler". Swiss art historian Sigfried Giedion dissents: "This backward turning of the head is in no way a tour de force arrived at because of limited material. . . . This type of head can frequently be found in Magdalenian art, even when ample space or material is at hand." Which authority shall we believe? To enjoy prehistoric art, it is not necessary to have a taste for controversy. But it helps.

Not all Cro-Magnon sculpture was as portable as the reindeer-antler bison. Some, like the wall paintings, is parietal art. Most of this stationary sculpture is bas-relief, and very little of it has survived the destructive effects of corrosion. That it has fared less well than the great cave paintings is probably due to its having been placed in more exposed locations where wind and water could get at it.

An imposing example is the sculptured animal frieze at Le Cap Blanc in the Dordogne. This remarkable work has been compared to the friezes of the Parthenon; today it is so badly damaged that at first sight the analogy seems farfetched (and no photograph does it justice). But close scrutiny of its parts bears out the comparison. Carved on the wall of a shallow rock shelter, the frieze is about 40 feet long. There are at least five horses, the largest of which is seven feet long, as well as a reindeer and traces of three small bison. When the frieze was first discovered in 1910, the animals, like the figures on the Parthenon, still showed vestiges of paint. Their positioning had been strongly influenced by the formation of the rock, and they appear to have been altered by Cro-Magnon artists at various times after they were first carved 15,000 to 16,000 years ago. Even so, it is clear that each in the succession of sculptors, working with burins and picks, exercised firm control over his work.

The overall effect is spacious and elegant. The arching backs of the animals, all appearing roughly on the same level, suggest a long, rolling ocean wave. The work is not formally organized, but nonetheless it has its own unity and represents a unique venture in art history: a sculptured pastoral landscape. Here the artists collaborated fully with nature, taking cues from shapes that already existed and developing them to suit their own uses, as a composer might elaborate on a given theme of music.

The prehistoric artist never isolated art in a picture frame or set it on a pedestal or in a pediment. Instead, he incorporated it into the environment. If, however, he found no rock formations that were useful to him, he constructed his own forms, as he did with the mating bison that adorn the cave at Le Tuc d'Audoubert in the Ariège region, near the Pyrénées (*page 129*). Here the artist apparently carved the two animals out of blocks of dry clay, a highly unusual procedure, for it involved adding a new substance to the rock setting. But he anchored his beasts so convincingly to the sloping rock surface that they seem a natural part of the environment.

The most majestic fusing of art and nature was found at Altamira in the great parietal paintings that the scholars turned their backs on. In due time, of course, the authenticity of the pictures was established, but it was a gradual process, dependent on a number of subsequent discoveries.

A turning point came in 1895 with the discovery in France—again through the curiosity of a youngster —of the cavern of La Mouthe, which included a ceiling decoration of bison. This time the experts were less sceptical; among those influencing the change of opinion were the same Edouard Piette who had tutored Don Marcelino de Sautuola at the time of the 1878 Paris Exhibition and later supported the Don's statements about the Altamira paintings. Piette noticed important similarities between La Mouthe

This elegant leaping horse from Bruniquel, France, was discovered some 15,000 years after it was carved from a reindeer antler. Though identified by some experts as a spear thrower, its delicate workmanship and small size—about a foot long—suggest that it was made for ceremonial use.

paintings and the Altamira art; with the discovery of more and more cave paintings at Font-de-Gaume and Les Combarelles in France, the French woke up to the fact that there was indeed a closely related body of cave art reaching from southwestern France to northwestern Spain.

The vindication of Altamira had begun. It was officially completed when Emile Cartailhac, one of the leading Altamira doubters, admitted his error in a now-famous article, "Mea Culpa d'un Sceptique," published in 1902. The next year, Cartailhac invited a young French priest, Henri Breuil, who had already made a name for himself as a specialist in Cro-Magnon studies, to go with him to Altamira. They carefully explored the caves, and Breuil began making his copies of the paintings that made the world aware of Cro-Magnon artistry.

The scholars who began pouring into the Altamira Cave, assessing its treasure and taking its measurements, reported that the main picture gallery, as it is now known, is only about 60 feet long, and 27 to 30 feet wide. The oppressively low ceiling makes it easy to understand why the ice-age artists chose to paint the ceiling rather than the walls. True, the ceiling is knobby with rocks; yet it may have been exactly this rough surface that appealed to the artists, because by painting animals over the protuberances they could achieve a more three-dimensional effect.

With a characteristic lack of unanimity, the experts have numbered the animals in the Altamira picture gallery from 25 to about 100, depending on whether they list each dim trace of an older animal over which some newer animal has been painted. A large majority of the beasts thus represented were life-sized. The picture gallery contains the works of several chronological periods. There is no agreement on dating. According to German archaeologist Johannes Maringer, the Aurignacian period (from about 21,000 to 34,000 years ago) is represented by outline paintings, small in size, simple in contour—what nowadays would be called line drawings. For about 2,000 years afterwards, the artists produced animal pictures with the bodies filled in with red or black. Then, in the full flower of later Magdalenian art (from 12,000 to 19,000 years ago), the emphasis veered towards drawing and shading inside the figure. Details of anatomy were picked out by heavy markings. Muscles appeared to swell, thanks to subtle gradations of colour.

All the colours used by the ancient artists were manufactured from natural earth pigments that, being minerals, are permanent. The most common was ochre, an earthy clay that contains iron minerals, giving it a range of hues from clear red and yellow to deep or tawny browns. Some blacks were made from charcoal, but the most permanent derived from manganese oxide, a fairly common material. All these colouring substances were reduced to a fine powder and then mixed with any of a number of lubricants, including blood, animal fat, urine, fish glue, egg white or vegetable juices.

From fragments of artists' gear found in caves it is even possible to conjecture the scene during a painting session. Conceivably, two or three artists worked together, the most experienced being the master, the others serving as assistants or apprentices, taking care of the lamps, pigments and other equipment.

The artists work entirely by artificial light provided by little cuplike lamps hollowed out of stone and fed with grease. They are placed around the cave on

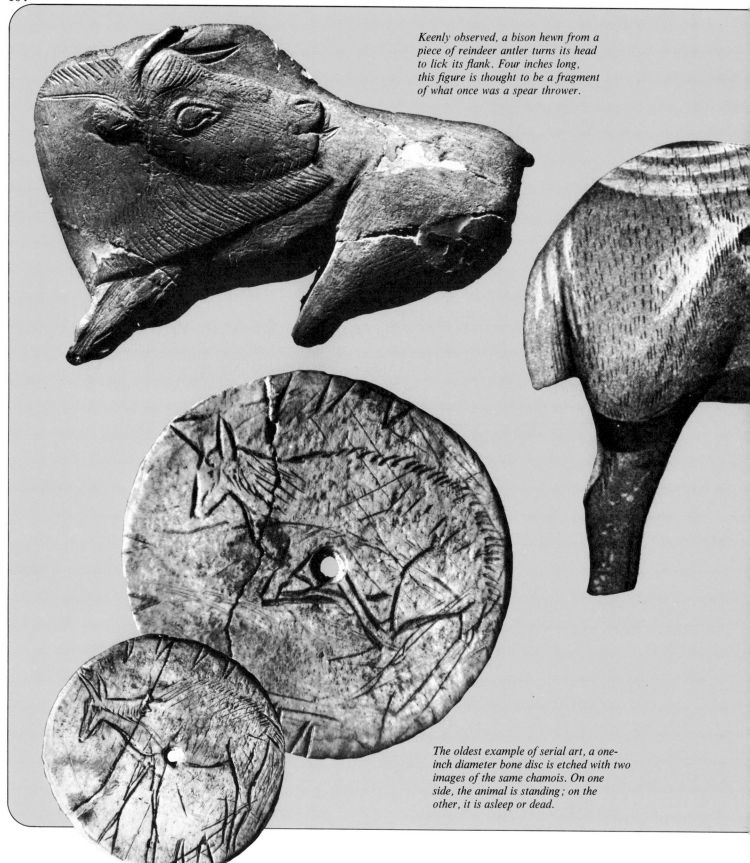

Keenly observed, a bison hewn from a piece of reindeer antler turns its head to lick its flank. Four inches long, this figure is thought to be a fragment of what once was a spear thrower.

The oldest example of serial art, a one-inch diameter bone disc is etched with two images of the same chamois. On one side, the animal is standing; on the other, it is asleep or dead.

A sliver of bone seven and three quarters inches long provided material for what was probably a spatula—in the shape of a salmon whose flaring tail served as a convenient handle.

Carved in mammoth ivory and only three inches long, this horse has a furry mane and coarse coat suggested by minute scratches neatly arranged in patterned rows all over its body.

Cro-Magnon's Brilliant Sculpture

Although painting, not carving, first brought Cro-Magnon man acclaim in the modern world as an artist, he knew how to sculpt and etch as well, infusing realism, spirit and style into chunks of horn or bone. The pieces that survive are tiny (hence the technical name mobiliary, or portable, art); the largest of these four, the elongated fish at right, is less than eight inches long. Many pieces are pierced to be worn on a thong; the disc (*left*) may have been a button. Almost all Cro-Magnon carvings depict animals, a natural choice for men who lived on beasts; and yet whatever the artists' practical concerns, they never failed to see— or capture—the inherent beauty of their subjects.

rocks and ledges, like altar lights. At other times and places lamps might consist of sea shells from the near-by coast, or bowls made out of skulls. Locks of hair or moss serve as wicks.

The dancing fires throw shadows on the walls and ceiling, and the air is heavy with burning fats—not to mention the vapours from gluey binders in the pigments—as the master artist consults a little sketch that he has previously made on a small slab of stone. (A few such slabs have been found, showing in miniature almost line for line the same animals that are pictured in certain caves.) As a final precaution before he starts work, he presses his hand against the ceiling area where he is going to paint, simply to test for moisture; the pigment must not be applied unless the rock is quite dry. His first job is to draw a simple outline of the animal, either with an engraving tool or in black pigment. If he uses pigment, he selects a paintbrush made of animal hair, although he might also use an oiled stick or a kind of crayon made of paste hardened into a handy lump.

Once the outline is drawn, the master proceeds to fill in the colours and accent certain details in black, such as eyes, horns, muscles and hoofs. He mixes his colours in separate sea-shell "paint jars" (a number of shells stained with shades of ochre have been found buried in cave strata) and uses a variety of devices for applying the colour. He may spread pigment gently with a brush and then smooth it with his fingers, or tamp it with a soft swab made from moss, lichen or fur until the shades blend together with almost imperceptible nuances. Or he may sprinkle it on as powder, or blow it through a tubular bird bone so that it sprays onto the rock like mist.

Considering the limited palette at the artist's disposal—yellow, red, brown and black—it is surprising how varied and lifelike the colour appears. When the master emerges from the cave after his operations are finished, people gather to gaze upon him with awe. Whether or not they are allowed to see his artistry, they know he has performed a magical service for the benefit of the group, and already they are investing him with something of the mystery and wonder of a shaman, or priest.

After Altamira was given an official seal of authenticity it remained for nearly 40 years the world's foremost showplace of prehistoric art. Its painted ceiling was more widely publicized than any other such overhead decoration save Michelangelo's masterpiece in the Vatican. The Altamira gallery, in fact, was called the Sistine Chapel of the ice age. But since 1940 Altamira has had to share honours with another spectacular find, at Lascaux on the river Vézère in France. The circumstances of its discovery sound like another version of the Altamira story, involving a hunting dog and youngsters. This time, the dog fell into a hole created when a fir tree was uprooted in a storm. Again, the lost dog's whimpering led its owner, one of four lads out for a day's sport together, to widen the hole and slither down to a cave floor 25 feet below the surface. His cronies followed, lit matches and saw themselves encircled by horses, stags and bulls painted on the walls. The boys had the fun of keeping their secret four days before telling their schoolmaster. And four days later the great Abbé Breuil, who happened to be staying 25 miles away, took charge of the place. The discovery was made during the German occupation of France in World War II. It was not possible then to install the

Under scrutiny, the tangle of scratchings in the stone above can be deciphered to reveal a whole menagerie: horses, rhinos, reindeer, ibexes, a cat and a hart. Such stones seem to have served as sketch pads on which an artist first drew figures later to be painted on cave walls. After he had finished transferring the figure onto the wall, the artist apparently obliterated the sketch by smearing it with ochre or mud; when that dried, he could begin another picture. What survives, with the coatings gone, is a jumble of overlaid outlines.

necessary air conditioning and heavy steel doors to keep the great system of cave walls protected. But by 1948 these installations had been made, Lascaux was opened to scholars and tourists, and it was visited daily by thousands.

For some reason unique to Lascaux, the human deluge was not salubrious. Algae began to attack the paints. The cave was closed while scientists figured out how to get rid of the menace, which seemed to be caused by human breath or other bodily exudations. The cure entailed getting rid of the people. Now the caves are open by appointment to only four or five people a day, most of them scientists.

Inevitably, Lascaux and Altamira invite comparison. Both caves were in use during roughly the same period, from about 12,000 to 34,000 years ago. But some scholars believe that the finest work at Altamira was done towards the end of this span, while the Lascaux painting was at its prime a few millennia earlier. The overall impression at Altamira is one of magical grandeur and repose. Bison, then the lords of the animal kingdom, dominate the congregation, huge parliamentary figures with their pelts hunched over their shoulders like fringed robes of ceremony. As Breuil described them, they are "sometimes simply standing resting, sometimes lying down or stretching, sometimes strolling lazily, sometimes galloping". But the gallopers are few. That the artists have endowed the beasts with nobility suggests something about the relationship between man and beast. Cro-Magnons may have looked up at these creatures with awe and respect, not yet having learned to treat the animal world with the indifference or condescension that men would one day adopt.

At least three of the Altamira bison are called re-

The two youthful discoverers of Lascaux Cave and its gallery of Cro-Magnon wall paintings, Marcel Ravidat and Jacques Marsal, stand at the cave's entrance with France's foremost prehistorian, Abbé Henri Breuil (in beret), and their proud schoolmaster. The boys and two friends explored a hole in the ground one autumn day in 1940 and came upon the paintings.

cumbent figures, their legs jack-knifed beneath them and their heads tucked low. A few authorities suggest that these are dying bison, with buckling legs. But the consensus is that they are asleep or giving birth. Their shapes seem to have been determined by protruding rocks, which lend themselves to this bunched-up position. Whatever the explanation —and different explanations may be correct for different examples—these giants are beautifully symbolic of energy coiled and waiting to spring forth from the earth.

For all its sober grandeur, the Altamira gallery has oddities and spontaneous outbursts. For example, "the bellowing bison" shatters the repose with his jaws open, his head pushed forward, his eyes wide with fury, his mane bristling like barbed wire and his whole back arched—perhaps the world's first portrait of rage. In total contrast, but just as unexpected, a peaceful bison with an uplifted head seems about to take a nibble from a leaf. Altamira boasts two boars, making it the only known cave in which a boar is unmistakably represented. Standing a bit aside, as if its dignity sets it apart, is a female red deer (*pages 116-117*); it is the largest painted animal (over seven feet long) in any Spanish cave. And scarcely noticed is the gentle, ghostlike head of a bison drawn in yellow perhaps 25,000 years ago. It is one of the oldest paintings in the cave, faded now, but still a mysteriously vivid presence.

In contrast, the Lascaux paintings (*pages 116, 118-119, 120-121*) are much less tranquil and much more variegated. Where Altamira's animals, for the most part, are relaxed and stately, the Lascaux beasts are often running wild; one famous rendering, known as the falling horse, is head-over-hoofs upside down.

Where the Altamira artists had a firm control of colour and movement, the Lascaux painters applied pigments loosely and used wavy lines that are almost baroque in their swirl and dash. Where Altamira appears classic and orthodox, Lascaux is freewheeling and, to modern viewers, exotic.

Lascaux is roughly a U-shaped cavern, about 330 feet end to end. Visitors enter through two massive metal barriers and soak their feet (with shoes on) in a pan of liquid disinfectant to kill any algae they might track in. Then they are allowed into the picture rotunda, where the first figure they see on the left wall, as if it were a guardian at the entrance, is a phantasmic beast. It fits appropriately into Lascaux's carnival of animals. Though called a unicorn, it is more of a "duocorn", possessing two straight horns that project in front. There is evidence that it was superimposed on an earlier work, perhaps a small horse in red outline. This oddly theatrical creature, about five feet six inches long, has also been described as having the body of a rhinoceros and the head of a Tibetan antelope. But it suggests the body of a masked man rigged up for a ceremony; the rings painted on its side, marking never observed on any natural creature, call to mind a masquerade costume. To set it further apart from nature, it has a square muzzle, a hump and is pregnant.

The dominating figures of the rotunda are four gigantic white bulls, each about 13 feet long and heavily outlined in black. No white pigment is used at Lascaux, but the effect is cleverly simulated by leaving the pale rock unpainted inside the black outlines. The impression of whiteness lends a mystical divinity to these beasts, similar to that of the white bull-god, Apis, of ancient Eygpt. The four bulls, in fact, might

Text continued on page 114

A Dramatic Cure for the "Green Sickness"

Lascaux's "unicorn"—so named despite its two horns—was one of the animals most affected by the algae. The wires are detectors to warn of the appearance of even microscopic algae spores.

One day in 1960, 20 years after the discovery of France's Lascaux Cave and its magnificent Cro-Magnon paintings, a frequent visitor to the cave noticed on a wall a tiny patch of green that had not been there before. Suspecting something malevolent, he revisited the cave over several weeks and, to his dismay, observed that the patch was growing; *maladie verte*, or green sickness, as it came to be called, threatened to engulf all Lascaux's treasured murals.

Immediately the cave was closed and scientists were enlisted to analyse the evil growth. Possibly, they speculated, the *maladie* consisted of algae that could flourish only in lighted places; total darkness might stem their spread. But darkness did no good; the *maladie* still proliferated.

Working against time in their laboratory, two biologists studied samples scraped from the walls. The growth, they found, was indeed an alga, one called *Palmellococcus*, which thrived on bacteria and mineral salts brought inadvertently into the cave by visitors. To stop its spread, the scientists sprayed the cave walls with a mixture of antibiotics—penicillin, streptomycin and kanamycin. And, as a final step, they applied a bath of formaldehyde and detergent to destroy the algae without leaving any disfiguring stains. So treated, the paintings are now infection-free and as unmarred as the day they were found (*overleaf*).

Protected in an airtight suit and face mask, a scientist saturates a cranny of Lascaux Cave with a high-pressure spray of antibiotic solution to kill the bacteria that nourish green algae.

Photomicrographs of a patch of algae-infected wall trace the cure: before treatment (top picture); shortly after (centre); and four months later (bottom), with the algae entirely gone.

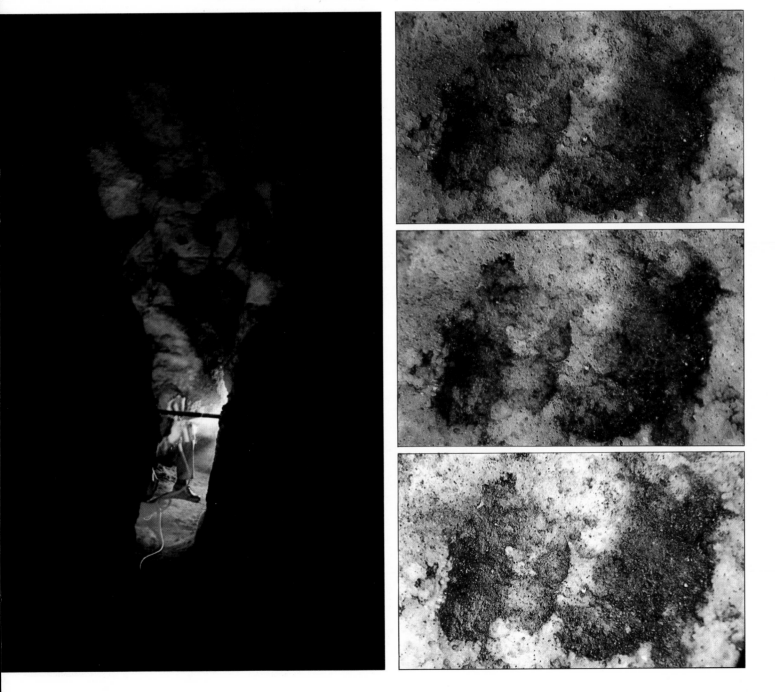

The murals inside the main hall at Lascaux today bear no traces of the infectious algae that long threatened to obliterate them. Even t

...ce severely afflicted unicorn (far left), following the animal cavalcade towards the cave's entry, is clearly visible.

be deities, benignly presiding over a universe of smaller animals: trotting horses, weirdly antlered deer, lesser cows. In the rotunda, as elsewhere in the cave, there are surprising differences in scale. Between the big bulls' legs is a frolicking jumble of smaller animals, a thicket of shanks and antlers. Here is an interplay of time and focus, a combination of ghostly creatures from the past, vanishing like the grin on the Cheshire cat, double exposures, mystical signs and enigmatic rows of black dots.

In the narrow axial gallery, 66 feet long, that extends from the back of the rotunda, a visitor feels he is walking through a stampede of animals that seems to be thundering just above his head. Two groups of creatures are competing with each other on opposite walls. On the left-hand wall are four cows and three small, incompletely painted horses. On the right wall is a far more exciting composition, dominated by 13 horses. Among them are five little ones that look like Shetland ponies jogging bravely ahead while a colossal cow sails over them. Also on this wall are the two famous "Chinese" horses (*pages 116 and 118-119*), so called because their thin legs and fat bellies resemble those of horses in classical Chinese art.

The treasures of Lascaux are much more varied than those of Altamira. But the subject matter in both groups raises many puzzling questions. The paintings seem to concentrate on animals that were the Cro-Magnon hunters' prey—bison, horses, deer. These figures are generally depicted with consummate naturalism. But human figures are not; when included at all they are either stick drawings or such chimeras as a bird-headed man. The masters of the golden age of prehistoric art revealed themselves in *art mobilier*, rather than in paintings; it was only in the closing years of the last ice age, just before the invention of agriculture, that large numbers of humans were painted on rock walls (*pages 145-151*).

These odd facts have naturally led the experts to flights of speculation—the paintings have been interpreted as signs imbued with magic, symbols of ritual and mystic clues to the presumed nature of the universe. But about the primary meaning of Cro-Magnon artistry—on cave walls and other media as well—there can be no question. The creation of fine art, of a quality later men would be hard pressed to better, introduced a wholly new element into human life. Its connection with the animal needs of survival that had preoccupied men for so long was indirect. It aimed higher. Henceforth the loftiest pursuits of mankind would be concerned not with the physical but with the intellectual and spiritual.

The Underground Masterpieces of the First Artists

Handprints made over 10,000 years ago survive in France's Gargas cave.

Cro-Magnon man's greatest gift to the world of today is his vibrant cave art. Using only tools and materials that nature supplied—feathers, bits of fur, moss or chewed twigs as brushes, reed or bone blowpipes and pigments from the earth—he limned the animals he knew, and on which he depended for food and clothing. So great was his talent that he made them seem real, capturing them in all their solidity—fleeing, charging, wounded. Indeed, the very process of depicting them on a cave wall or ceiling may have seemed to him a way of gaining control over them—of inviting or ensuring his success on the hunt.

Abundant evidence of his work survives in some 100 European caves and rock shelters, and more is still coming to light (a cave discovered recently in Spanish Basque country contained paintings of horses and bison).

Locked away for centuries in tomb-like darkness, many of the images are as fresh as they were the day they were created; some of the most brilliant—in Lascaux, Niaux and Rouffignac caves in France, and Altamira in Spain—are reproduced on the following pages. Who created them no one will ever know. For all Cro-Magnon's brilliance as an artist, the closest he ever came to "signing" his work was to leave occasional handprints on cave walls—often made, like those shown here, by stencilling around the fingers with pigment.

Lascaux: A painted horse, its slim limbs outstretched, seems to be running.

Niaux: Sketched boldly in black pigment, a long-haired horse radiates energy.

A life-sized doe, gracefully and accurately proportione

...dorns the cave's ceiling. The artist used delicate colouring and fine lines to emphasize the animal's curves.

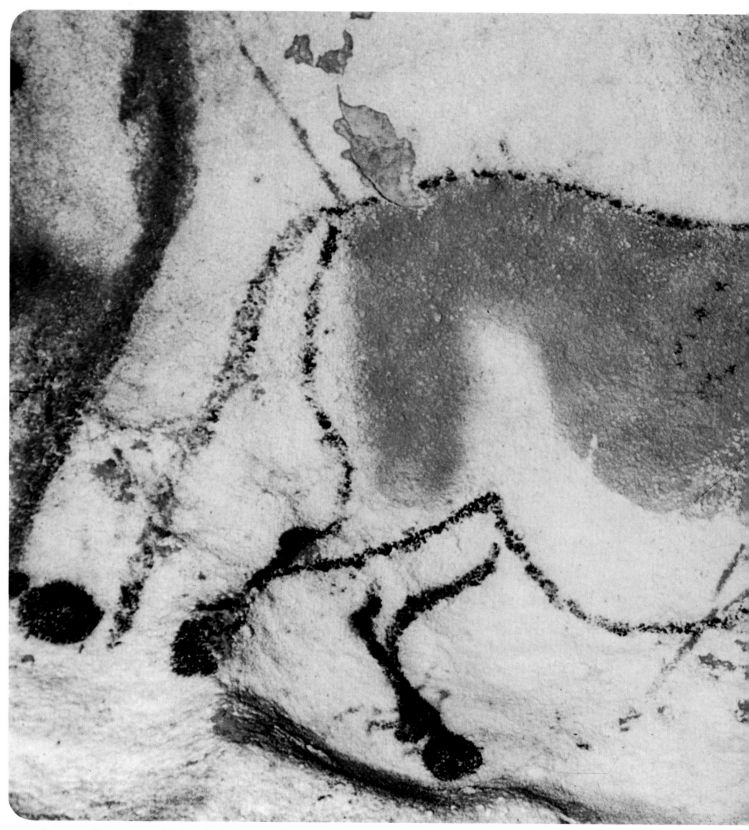

Lascaux: Reminiscent of Oriental art because of its graceful, compact shape, this galloping animal is often referred to as the "Chinese" hors

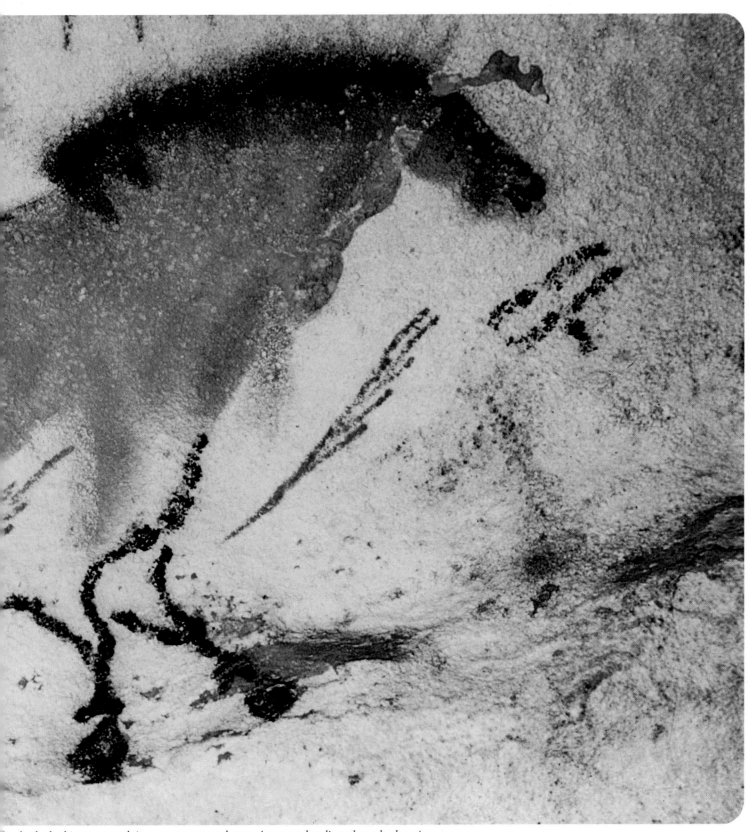

he barbed objects around it may represent hunters' spears hurtling through the air.

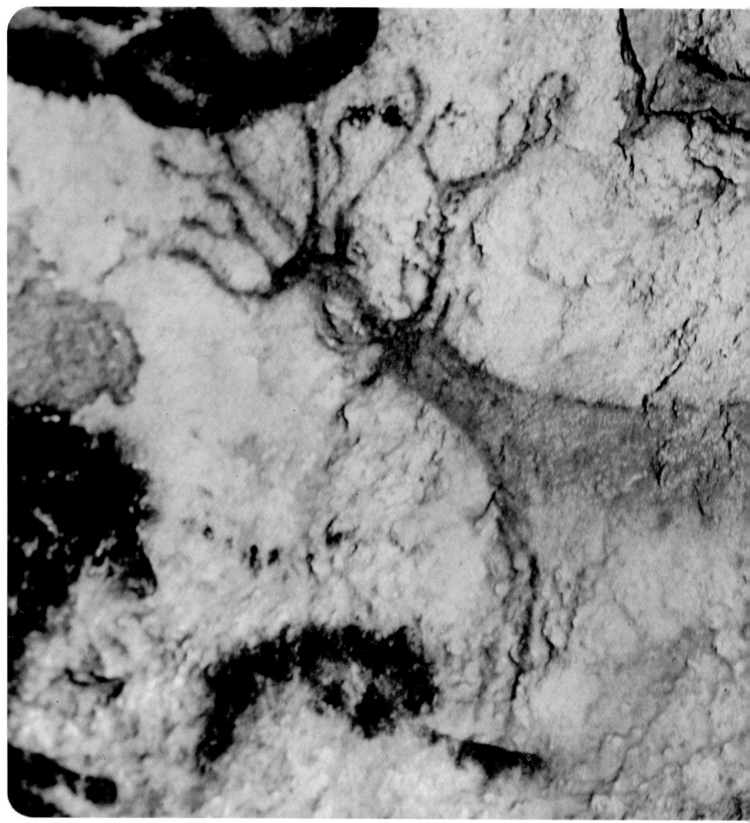

Lascaux: Three deer in rapid flight are silhouetted in different-coloured pigments on the wall of the cave complex's main entrand

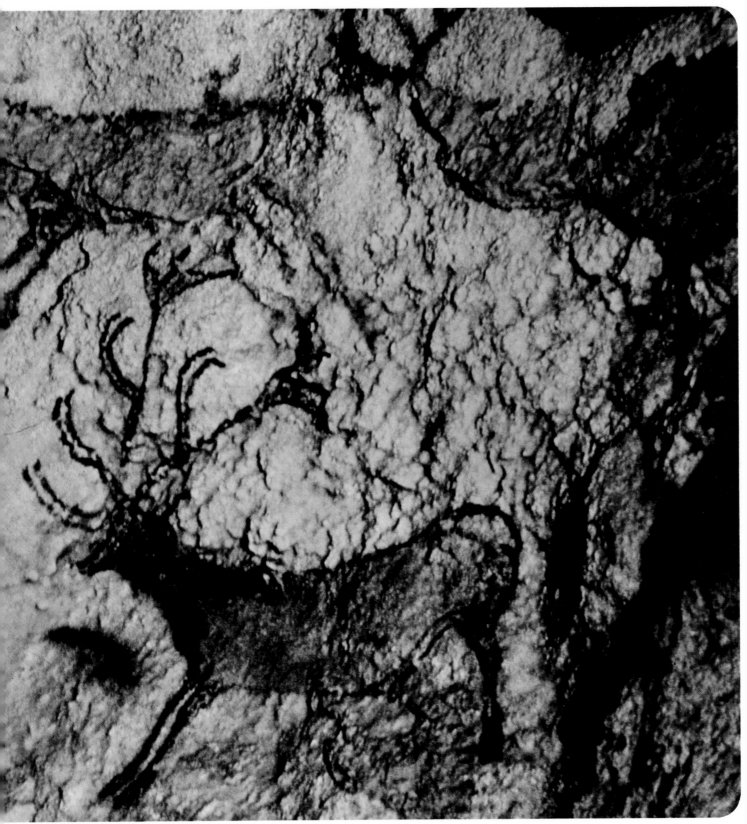

...eer, a common subject in Cro-Magnon art, turn up 14 times on Lascaux's walls.

Niaux: Pockmarks in the clay floor, made by water dripping from the ceiling, have been incorporated into a profile view of an injur

son. The addition of a few strokes around the circular depressions suggests that the animal's wounds are spurting blood.

Niaux: A bison painted on a wall seems about to charge an aggressor. Its shaggy coat is rendered in fine detail.

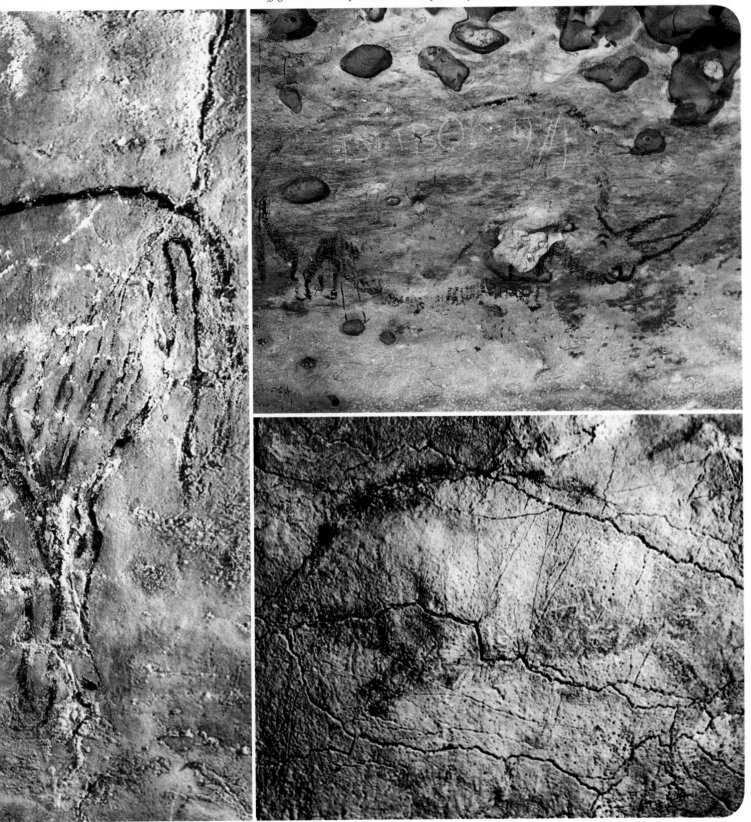

Rouffignac: A woolly rhinoceros—defaced by a visitor—is so fat that it drags its stomach.

Altamira: One of the fiercest of Stone Age animals, a life-sized boar, leaps through space.

Chapter Five: The Subtle Mind of Cro-Magnon

Cro-Magnon's anatomy was modern, his intelligence keen, his technical skills well developed, his art masterful. What of his mind, his spirit? Did he have any way of recording his feelings about nature? What did his paintings indicate beyond his considerable aesthetic sensitivity? Did they represent beliefs in the supernatural? Homage to mystical powers? Rituals of magic? Did he have a religion? The answers must be speculative, to be sure, and prehistorians will always argue the fine points. But there is no doubt that one vital phase in man's intellectual development had been achieved by Cro-Magnon's time: the capacity for symbolic behaviour.

Symbols are the key to man's mental and spiritual outlook; alphabets, words, numbers, calendars, pictures, cathedrals are all symbols that convey meaning other than their own reality. The antlered headdress of a Cro-Magnon leader, such as that of the shaman or sorcerer shown here, and the mitre of a bishop are both symbols of specialization and status. Ceremonies and rituals of all kinds are symbolic, be they political, religious or magical, and the altar candles in a modern church and the flickering oil lamps that lighted up the wall paintings in a Cro-Magnon cave are both adjuncts of symbolic drama.

Caves are a natural breeding ground for magic. Certainly to anyone who has penetrated more than a few steps into a prehistoric cave, there is an aura of mystery in the bulging walls and ceilings and the dark,

Ceremoniously attired in animal skins and stag antlers, a figure from Les Trois-Frères Cave in southern France appears here in a drawing done in 1912 by Abbé Breuil, dean of Cro-Magnon studies. This figure, interpreted by Breuil as that of a shaman, is among a small number of paintings that provide clues to the symbolic behaviour of the first modern men.

looming recesses. By lamplight they are alive with fanciful shapes and shadows. Each cave has its own special character, its own mood—from the chapel-like compactness of the main chamber at Altamira to the long twisting alleys of Les Combarelles and the strangely inviting alcoves and passages of Font-de-Gaume. But in common, most possess sequestered areas that might have served for some sort of ceremonies or rites, or as shrines. A few of these spots are extremely difficult to reach, suggesting that in prehistoric times they may have been considered all the more sacred for being located in nearly inaccessible crannies or shafts.

Some archaeologists have surmised that these hidden sanctuaries were chosen for primitive initiation rites. Cro-Magnon neophytes may have had to crawl through dark, moist tunnels, terrified of getting lost, perhaps faint from fasting, to be rewarded finally with a glimpse by dim lamplight of a painted animal or some other magical image. Although there is no solid evidence of such initiations in prehistoric times, such ceremonies in similarly impressive settings have been a part of human existence as far back as any written record goes. And there is every likelihood that a lively-minded people, like the Cro-Magnons, very much under the sway of nature, subject to fears and vicissitudes both imagined and real, would make use of their caves in dramatic ways.

One of the most melodramatic settings for an initiation is near the foothills of the French Pyrénées, where two adjacent cave systems comingle with the little river Volp. Both caves are on the estate of the late Count Henri Bégouën, an archaeologist on the faculty of the University of Toulouse. The Count had three sons. It should hardly surprise the reader, then, that the boys figured prominently in the caves' discovery. They had heard that the river led to a maze of underground chambers and corridors. One summer day in 1912, they entered the opening in a hillside into which the Volp flowed and, with a raft they had built of petrol cans, began to explore the cave.

As if navigating the river Styx into the underworld, they rounded a few bends and drifted into a large dark gallery, where they left their raft on a little gravel beach. Then, holding lanterns, they walked into a passage about 70 feet long, eventually reaching a hall with a pool in it. This room was subsequently called the Bridal Chamber because of its lacy white stalagmites and stalactites. At the end of the Bridal Chamber they clambered up a steep 40-foot slope and hacked down stalactites to gain entrance to a tunnel, which they followed for several hundred yards. After squeezing through a low, narrow section they reached another hall strewn with what turned out to be the fossilized bones of cave bears, and finally, near the end of the cave complex, they entered a circular room. Here they came upon a stunning sight, almost frightening in the sharply shadowed light of their lanterns: two bison handsomely modelled of dried clay, each approximately two feet long, propped up against a rock fallen from the roof (*page 129*).

To the sons of Count Bégouën, their adventure had much of the excitement and mystery of an initiation rite, and to the Count himself, when he inspected the find, it seemed that the cave was probably used for just such purposes. In the fine clay floor of an alcove near the bison room, the Count and his fellow archaeologists discovered some 50 human heel prints, preserved by a thin crust of calcite. Judging by their relatively small size, they were made by five or six children, ranging in age from 13 to 15. Of course, the small heel prints may have been left only by curious youngsters exploring the cave. But on the floor near the heel prints the explorers found several clay "sausages", presumed to be little phalluses. This almost inaccessible alcove, deep underground, was possibly a scene of fertility rites, a place where boys kept vigils. Concern for the reproduction of bison would be natural among people who depended on such large and powerful animals for sustenance and hides.

Two years after discovery of the bison room, the Count and his sons began to explore a second cave, which was connected to the first, and which in the boys' honour he named Les Trois-Frères, The Three Brothers. Once again they found strong evidence of magic in a hard-to-reach spot. Beginning the usual obstacle course, they crawled down holes and up slopes, sidled through a passage guarded by painted and engraved lions' heads, and entered a bell-shaped alcove in the bowels of the earth.

Here they saw on the walls a network of engraved pictures of various beasts, drawings resting as lightly on the rock as cobwebs. This art amounts to a magical zoo. A female reindeer has the front quarters of a heavy-set bison. Herding the animals is a hybrid creature with human legs, a tail and horned head, dancing and playing what appears to be a flute or some other kind of musical instrument. Inevitably this figure calls to mind the jigging satyrs and Pans of early Greek mythology.

But the most arresting figure is at the top of the alcove, presiding as if he were a Lord of the Beasts keeping watch over his bizarre flock (*page 126*). With his helmet of antlers, his hypnotic owlish eyes, his

Two 24-inch-long clay bison lean against a limestone block in a remote chamber of Le Tuc d'Audoubert Cave near Ariège, France. The figures, possibly used in rites of some kind, survived 15,000 years practically undamaged by moisture and temperature changes that ruined more-exposed sculptures.

An enigmatic painting in Lascaux Cave depicts a man with a bird's head, a bird on a rod, a disembowelled bison and, to the left, a rhinoceros. The location of the picture at the bottom of a shaft suggests that it was deliberately painted in a hard-to-reach place, possibly in connection with an initiation rite.

horse's tail, wolf's ears, bear's front paws and what look like the feet and sexual organs of a man, he is a creature of electrifying vitality, a magical amalgam of animal and human forces. One of the masterpieces of Cro-Magnon art, he has often been called a sorcerer or shaman.

There is no direct evidence in their art that the Cro-Magnon people practiced shamanism, but because of the presence of such chimeras as the ambiguous Lord of the Beasts at the cave of Les Trois-Frères, many archaeologists have speculated on the possibility. In addition, there is the Bird-Man of Lascaux, suitably inaccessible at the bottom of a 23-foot shaft. Crudely painted, his body resembles a string bean with matchstick legs and arms (*page 130*). He has only four fingers on each hand. His beaked head is uplifted. Beside him are an odd assortment of props: a bird-headed post or rod (which may in fact represent a spear thrower) and a mighty barbed pike leaning against a huge bristling bison, mortally wounded, with loops of entrails spilling from its belly. A few feet away is an enigmatic rhinoceros, tail uplifted, seemingly unconcerned by the uproar.

According to the noted interpreter of Cro-Magnon art, Abbé Breuil, this painting is simply a violent hunting scene in which the man has mangled the bison and in turn has been killed by the rhino. Breuil was so sure that the picture recorded an actual hunting tragedy that he dug in the shaft to see if the hunter's bones had been buried near his picture. No such bones were found.

Later experts saw the picture as a symbolic battle between three clans whose totemic emblems were the bird, the rhino and the bison. Others saw it as a clash of male and female symbols, the spear being male and the bison, with its intestines looped in supposedly womanly ovals, being female. A third, widely held theory is that the bird-headed man is a masked shaman, taking part in some ritual and toppling over in a trance. In support of the shaman theory, it has been pointed out that a bird, such as surmounts the stick/spear thrower, is often associated with shamans in modern Siberia.

The link with Siberia is perhaps significant. In the lives of primitive hunters living there today, the shaman is an important figure—a diviner, a healer, a sorcerer. In an ecstatic trancelike experience he predicts the future by the practice of magic. He also appears to extract the illness from the patient's body. To a people utterly dependent upon nature for survival, he gives a sense of knowing and doing something about their fate.

Whether such observations of the present can be extrapolated to the past is of course disputable. But there is no doubt that shamanism represents a significant example of symbolic behaviour among some hunter-gatherer peoples today, and its modern form —not only in Siberia but in South America, Africa and elsewhere—may suggest how prehistoric man thought about forces whose powers he acknowledged to be superior to his own.

To be a 20th Century shaman among Central Siberian hunters a man must have a line of shamans in the family. "The spirit of my deceased brother Ilya comes and speaks through my mouth," explained Semyonov Semyon, a practicing Tungus shaman of Mongolian descent, quoted in mythologist Joseph Campbell's *The Masks of God: Primitive Mythology*.

Physical suffering and a fantastic ordeal prepared Semyon for full shamanhood. "My ancestors began

Text continued on page 136

Cryptic Messages from the Past

Along with explicitly realistic pictures of bison, reindeer and other Stone Age beasts, Cro-Magnon men also left mysterious markings on the walls of caves, perhaps as parts of rituals. The oldest of these puzzling designs seem to be silhouettes of human hands. In Gargas Cave, in the French Pyrénées, almost 150 handprints, fingers outspread, are scattered over the walls. Still more cryptic are abstract patterns of coloured dots and lines in other caves; they could represent plant forms, human anatomy or some sort of man-made structure or implement.

The real meaning of such ancient graphics may never be revealed, although there is no lack of interpretations, ranging from the serious to the ridiculous. Various people at one time or another have seen them as casual doodling, prayers, traffic signs, coats-of-arms or sexual symbols.

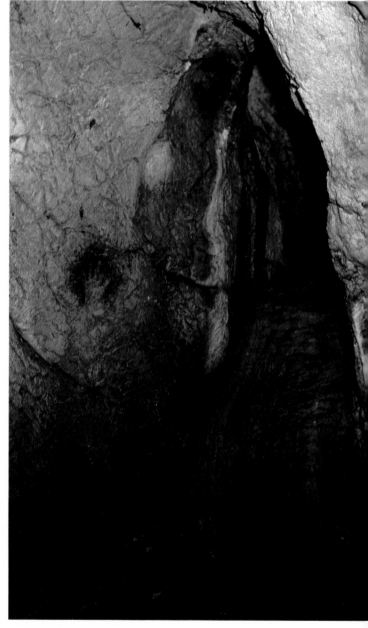

Snaking along a wall in Marsoulas Cave in southern France, a barbed line (right) looks like a plant, though similar signs have been read as feathers, arrows and stylized phalluses. In the adjacent photograph, a handprint placed just outside a passageway in Gargas Cave in the Pyrénées has been seen as a supplication to a spirit.

Geometric forms, like the one below from Altamira, were identified as dwellings by the noted Abbé Breuil, although they have also been called traps, coats-of-arms and shields.
Dots in rows, in the photograph at bottom at La Pileta, Spain, may represent calendar marks, route signs, trees or, in one improbable interpretation, "apples, cherries, raspberries and strawberries," painted to encourage a fruitful harvest.

Pelted with dots, a painting of two horses in France's Pech Merle Cave combines two kinds of symbols for what could be simple decoration or signs of hunting magic. The dots could represent projectiles; the handprints surrounding the horses, man's power over his prey. Taken together, the dots and hands would then be an invocation to the supernatural, intended to assure the hunters of a successful kill.

Rows of dots paired with boxes at El Castillo, Spain, are assigned a sexual meaning by French anthropologist André Leroi-Gourhan. The dots, he says, are male signs, the boxes female signs, and together they are symbols of a religion based on fertility.

Bell shapes and a barbed sign, also from the cave at El Castillo, were read as stylized male and female sex organs by Leroi-Gourhan; to him the paired symbols are manifestations of the same duality as the Chinese yin and yang, or the Roman Jupiter and Juno.

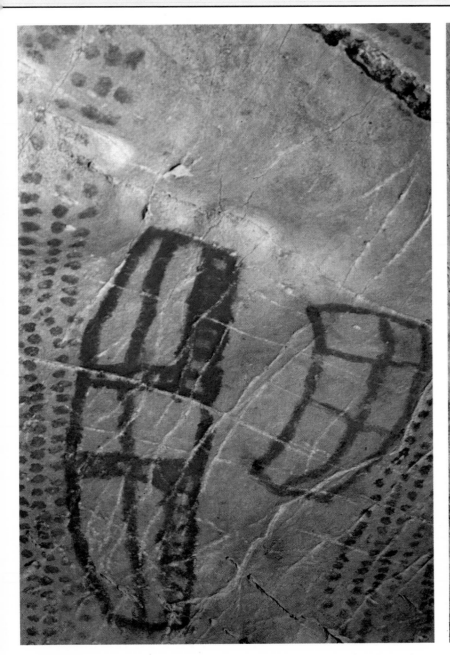

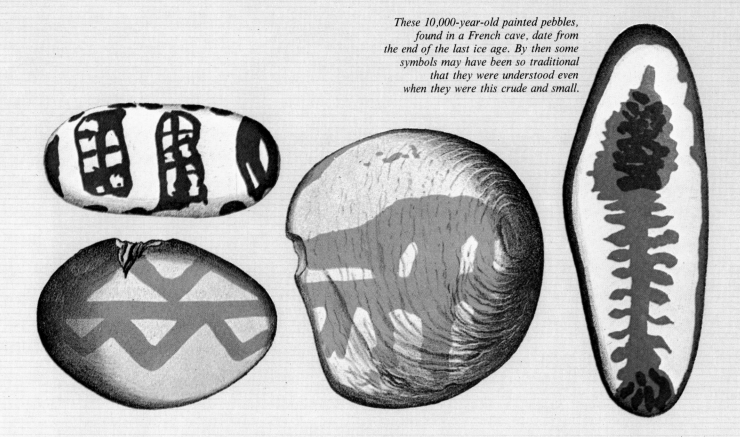

These 10,000-year-old painted pebbles, found in a French cave, date from the end of the last ice age. By then some symbols may have been so traditional that they were understood even when they were this crude and small.

to shamanize with me. They stood me up like a block of wood and shot at me with their bows until I lost consciousness. They cut up my flesh, separated my bones, counted them, and ate my flesh raw. . . . And while they were performing this rite, I ate and drank nothing the whole summer. But at the end the shaman spirits drank the blood of a reindeer and gave me some to drink, too. . . . The same thing happens to every Tungus shaman. Only after his shaman ancestors have cut up his body in this way and separated his bones can he begin to practice."

Though elements of myth, hallucination and humbug are obscurely tangled in this account, it testifies clearly to the dedication and mystical involvement that go with ancient shamanist tradition.

Only rarely have shamans' feats been witnessed by trained observers. A remarkable report, often quoted in literature on shamanism, was made by Lucas Bridges, son of a missionary, who spent his early years among the Ona people, hunters in Tierra del Fuego. At this storm-lashed outpost on the southernmost tip of South America, several 20th Century tribes of Indians, whose ancestors probably crossed to the New World from Siberia during Cro-Magnon times, carried on a way of life that appeared substandard even by Stone Age standards. Bridges relates his experience one bright, moonlit night with a shaman called Houshken.

Houshken began with a chant that eventually led him into a trance. "Drawing himself up to his full height, he took a step towards me," reports Bridges, "and let his robe, his only garment, fall to the ground. He put his hands to his mouth with a most impressive gesture and brought them away again with fists clenched and thumbs close together. He held them to the height of my eyes and, when they were less than two feet from my face, slowly drew them apart. I saw that there was now a small, almost opaque object between them. It was about an inch in diameter in the middle and tapered away into his hands. It might have been a piece of semitransparent dough or elastic, but whatever it was it seemed to be alive, revolving at great speed, while Houshken, apparently from muscular tension, was trembling violently. . . .

"As I gazed at this strange object, Houshken brought his hands further apart and the object grew more and more transparent until . . . I realized that it was not there anymore. It did not burst or break like a bubble; it simply disappeared, having been visible to me for less than five seconds. Houshken made no sudden movement, but slowly opened his hands and turned them over for my inspection. They looked clean and dry. He was stark naked and there was no confederate beside him. I glanced down at the snow, and, in spite of his stoicism, Houshken could not resist a chuckle, for nothing was to be seen there.

"The others had crowded around us and, as the object disappeared," Bridges continues, "there was a frightened gasp from among them. . . . The natives believed this to be an incredibly malignant spirit. . . . It might take physical form, as we had just witnessed, or be totally invisible. It had the power to introduce insects, tiny mice, mud, sharp flint, or even a jellyfish or baby octopus into the anatomy of those who had incurred its master's displeasure. I have seen a strong man shudder involuntarily at the thought of this horror and its evil potentialities."

The shaman's repertory of tricks and cures, aids and benefits varied greatly from one primitive culture to another, but it was always based on magic —on the notion of another reality. Man could hardly have progressed to science if he had not first been trained in magic, or made to wonder about what seemed beyond his understanding. Magic is the art of producing desired results through the use of various techniques—including symbols, signs and rites —that presumably guarantee the magician control over the forces of nature or of the supernatural. Magic is, in a sense, make-believe science. It involves procedures that in themselves may be preposterous; nonetheless, they suggest ways and means of getting things done, rough methodologies for later advances. Magic was an invaluable therapy that inspired and fortified primitive man, combating his fear of death and forces beyond his control and building up his confidence. To the hunter especially, magic was an auxiliary weapon, nearly as essential as his spear —and if it failed, then something must have been wrong with the way the magic had been conducted, or something more powerful must have intervened.

The magic ceremonies of the Cro-Magnons are of course unrecorded. But the evidence of magic is seen by many experts in Cro-Magnon art. The paintings, engravings, bas-reliefs and figurines are widely interpreted as equivalents of Houshkin's magically disappearing object—symbols intimately associated with ritual and the supernatural.

There are, for example, representations of hands that occur in more than 20 caves in Spain, Italy and France. Hardly classifiable as art, they seem to be tokens of human presence, like thumbprints or footprints. Some are silhouettes, others have been traced and then painted in, still others are just outlines.

What do they signify? Why do left hands far outnumber right in some caves? Are they related to a system of counting? Or a census? Do they, in cases where only some of the fingers are shown, represent ritual mutilations or a kind of sign language, perhaps symbols for animals? The Bushmen of South Africa use hand signals to identify the various animals they spot when out hunting.

Many such questions and speculations have been seriously advanced. But the hands do not communicate. Still, seeing them in a shadowy cave, such as Gargas in France, is a strangely moving experience. They are the next thing to a flesh-and-blood link to our own remote ancestors, waving to us across thousands of years.

Another presumably magic symbol encountered scattered among cave paintings is the tectiform, from the Latin root meaning roof. These "roofed" forms, often rectangular with several crossbeams, resemble scaffolds of some sort and may in fact be the first man-made structures ever depicted (*page 135*). But, then, what are they? Huts? Tents? Dwellings for spirits? Traps set for animals?

Not all authorities now interpret prehistoric art as signs of magic, however. Some who are influenced by the works of Sigmund Freud, notably France's André Leroi-Gourhan, have interpreted almost all cave painting within yet another framework—that of a complex system of sexual symbolism.

Leroi-Gourhan took a massive inventory of cave art and found that only a small part of it seemed to be concerned with ritual on behalf of the hunt. In his view Cro-Magnon art was shaped instead by a strong awareness of the different sexes, an awareness that at times was downright explicit. Male and female each had its own symbols, animals, objects and so on, which Leroi-Gourhan felt split practically the whole world into male and female camps. Animals in the male group included deer, ibex, bears and rhinoceros; in the female group, bison and wild cattle. Among the abstract signs that punctuate almost all examples of cave art, Leroi-Gourhan used a Freudian system to classify points, barbs and batons as male, and ovals, triangles and rectangles as female. He determined which animals and designs are male and which female by noting which obviously sexual symbol they are near.

After examining more than 2,000 animal pictures and some 60 caves, Leroi-Gourhan reported that 90 per cent of the bison and wild cattle symbolizing females are bunched in the centre of caves, in the womb as it were, while 70 per cent of the abstract male symbols occupy the outposts, where they might function as some sort of hex signs. Thus, Leroi-Gourhan saw the cave as a paradigm of life on earth, played out like a dream of early man to affirm the balance of nature. He suggested that this meaning may go well beyond the balancing of male and female principles, and include the harmonization of all opposing forces, an abstract concept similar to the yin and yang in Oriental philosophy.

This theory, predictably, has elicited a storm of criticism. Its attackers say it presupposes that such caves as Altamira and Lascaux were planned by Cro-Magnons in advance to accommodate a balanced distribution of sex symbols, whereas much evidence indicates that these caves were decorated at random and over the years—and even over centuries.

One great obstacle to understanding the images and designs created by the people of Cro-Magnon times has been the tendency to think of palaeolithic

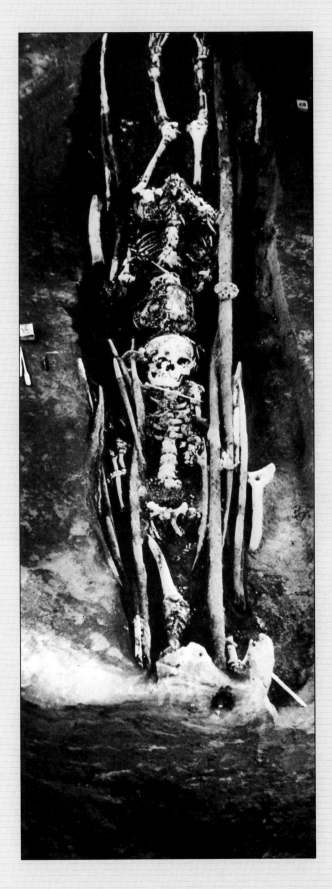

art, in all its ramifications, as a single body of material. In truth, it is enormously varied, containing many styles, and produced in many places over a period that is estimated to have been as long as 30,000 years. It is entirely plausible, then, that symbols such as hands and tectiforms had different meanings at different times. Even the cave sites, through many millennia, probably served diversely as council chambers, shrines, schools, archives, ritual theatres and vigil places.

There is more than art to suggest that the people of Cro-Magnon times were developing increasing sophistication in coping with the intangible fears, anxieties and mysteries that seem to have accompanied their growing awareness of their own intellect and consciousness. The fear of death, a questioning of what it means and what it leads to, has always been one of the most basic human concerns, one that the Cro-Magnons shared with other men.

That the Neanderthals believed in an afterlife before the Cro-Magnons was suggested by the discovery in France of the skeleton of a man who was buried with a funeral offering of meat. But from the unearthing of burial grounds in Russia, it is now clear that some Cro-Magnon peoples had far higher standards of funerary luxury than was commonly supposed, and accompanied the interments of their dead with symbolic rituals of unprecedented magnificence. It is possible that these trappings were meant to ensure a comfortable afterlife for the deceased, although it is also possible that they were symbols of earthly status meant to impress the living. In either case, they provide a new glimpse of Stone Age elegance and concern with death.

Notes from a Cro-Magnon Moon Watcher

Discovered over 50 years ago in a Cro-Magnon rock shelter in France's Dordogne region, a reindeer-antler plaque (shown above three and a half times its actual size) may bear one of man's oldest meaningful notations—the precursor of writing. According to a controversial theory proposed by Alexander Marshack, research associate at Harvard's Peabody Museum, the antler's puzzling marks represent a record of the phases of the moon.

Marshack was led to this startling hypothesis when microscopic examination of the plaque suggested that the marks were made one at a time over an extended period—and with different tools. He could distinguish several tool points and varying pressures. These variations indicated the serpentine line of marks was not a random design 'struck off at one sitting but rather a purposeful sequence. The marks seemed to be some sort of tally, and Marshack found that they could be roughly matched to the phases of the moon, as indicated at right.

If Marshack's theory is correct, it indicates that men were making written notations more than 30,000 years ago—25,000 years before the Sumerians invented cuneiform writing.

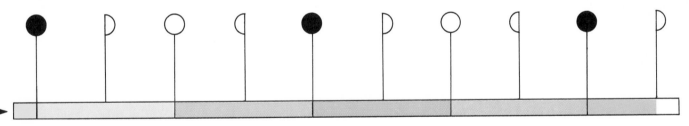

*A multicoloured band is superimposed on the Cro-Magnon
plaque above to colour-code its curving line of 69 marks; the
band is straightened in the accompanying diagram of
lunar phases to show how Alexander Marshack relates the
marks to the waxing and waning of the moon. The first mark
(arrow in photograph) corresponds to a night just before
the moon waned to invisibility (arrow in diagram).
Each succeeding mark represents another night, forming a
written lunar record. Its curved track may indicate the
changing position of the moonrise on successive evenings.*

The finds were made in two main instalments, both in a 23,000-year-old burial ground located in a region of permafrost, or permanently frozen ground, about 130 miles northeast of Moscow. The first dig, carried out in 1964, yielded the remains of two skeletons, the more complete of the two belonging to a man of about 55 who had been buried wearing lavishly beaded fur clothing (*page 34*). Before his burial his grave had been strewn with red ochre, and later the corpse itself was sprinkled with ochre, which, once the flesh had decayed, coated the bones of the skeleton in powdery scarlet.

Archaeologists guess that the red ochre was meant either to symbolize the blood of living men or to make the dead look more lifelike. Beneath and on top of the skeleton, about 1,500 bone ornaments were found, as well as pierced arctic fox canine teeth, presumably once forming part of a necklace, two dozen bracelets carved from mammoth ivory, and beads of the same material that had been sewed in rows on the man's leather clothes.

The second major find, unearthed in 1969, was even more spectacular. It included in one grave the skeletons of two boys, both on their backs, their legs pointing in opposite directions, their skulls almost touching (*page 139*). Head to head, they stretched out in one line. The younger boy was somewhere between seven and nine, the other about five years older. Besides their lavishly beaded garments, they were equipped with weapons, including eight-foot-long spears, made from straightened mammoth tusks, with very sharp, thin points. Both corpses wore ivory bracelets and rings, and there was evidence of headgear of some sort; long pins under their chins had been used for fastening the collars of their garments to keep them warm and snug. Next to the skeletons lay two *bâtons de commandement*.

No one knows whether all these appurtenances were to provide status for the boys in afterlife, or to warm and comfort their souls, or simply to honour the family's important position in earthly society. But whatever their purpose, they were clearly symbolic; the objects stood, in the eyes of the people who put them there, for something else, something that was important enough to expend a considerable amount of worldly wealth on. This is a practice that has claimed a good deal of man's energy and riches in the millennia since.

A further indication of Cro-Magnon's intellectual progress came in 1962, and it came from outside the field of formal archaeology. It raises the possibility that these ancient people were using symbols in a way that, at a much later date, would lead to writing. The discovery was made by Alexander Marshack, who is now a research associate at Harvard's Peabody Museum but was then a science writer preparing a book on NASA's lunar programme. Seeking material on the origins of science, he came across a photograph of a small 8,000-year-old bone artifact with an orderly sequence of grooves and scratches on its sides. Marshack knew that such nicks were fairly common on prehistoric bones and stones. But now it struck him that such marks, instead of being ornamental or, as sometimes assumed, a tally of animals killed, might represent some sort of notations. He found that the 167 marks on the bone could be a record of the phases of the moon, made over an approximately six-month period.

Putting aside the book he was writing on space,

Marshack began a four-year project that involved him in a microscopic scrutiny of hundreds of engraved Stone Age artifacts. There were suggestive nicks on many of them, but on objects from the Aurignacian period, 34,000 years ago, there appear what seem to be an unusually large number of highly complex notational markings. Marshack focused on about 30 well-preserved pieces that he felt might—like the 8,000-year-old bone that had started him on his quest —also represent phases of the moon.

The most impressive was an oval plaque, carved from antler and found in the Dordogne region of France (*pages 140-141*). On one face, the artisan had formed a serpentine band composed of 69 clearly distinguishable marks. As Marshack examined the plaque still more closely, he became convinced that this could not be a casual decoration done by a Cro-Magnon at one or two sittings. The microscope made it clear that whoever made the 69 marks had changed his pointed tool, as well as his pressure and style of stroke, 24 different times.

The markings, Marshack points out, are on a very small scale. So if one were merely trying to decorate this small space, it is likely that the engraver would have made each mark with the sharp point of the same tool, using a similar style of stroke and a similar amount of pressure. But this, as Marshack saw through his microscope, was not the case. It is unlikely that the carver would choose to change points so frequently, so Marshack assumed that the notations were built up sequentially at different times with different tools.

This conclusion in turn suggested that the marks were some kind of systematic notation, which the artisan was making for himself or perhaps his group.

Blades for a Sickle

One of the last great developments in stone toolmaking techniques in the Old World was the geometric microlith—a small piece of angled flint, frequently broken from a larger, sharp-edged blade like the one shown at top. When notched and snapped into three pieces, as in the second row, such a blade yielded a centre portion that had a trapezoid shape (the other two sections are waste) or, as in the bottom row, one with a triangular or crescent shape. These microliths could then be fitted—their sharp edges out—into a wooden or bone handle and held in place with pine pitch or some other kind of primitive glue. The resultant tool (below) made an efficient saw or sickle which could be used for such tasks as cutting grass for bedding and shelters or even for gathering heads of wild grains.

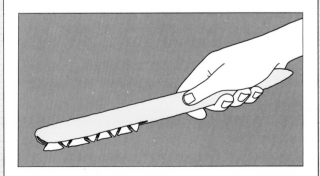

Marshack deduced that each mark signified a different night, and that the snaky track with its odd twists and turns was a schematic representation of the moon's rising and setting points over a two-and-one-quarter-month period.

To an observer looking south, after the night of the first crescent, the growing, or waxing, moon is first seen further eastward and higher each night until the seventh night, when the moon is at its highest point. But on the eighth day the moon begins to dip in the sky, the eastward progression continuing for 15 days, until the moon is full. On the fifteenth day, the process reverses and the moon begins to grow smaller. Each turn in the curving track on the bone thus corresponds roughly to a time in the month when the moon begins a major change of phase—either waxing or waning. At such a point the moon begins to reverse its place and time of first appearance. If Marshack's interpretation is correct, it would mean that the Cro-Magnons were capable of gathering information and recording it at regular intervals.

Some scholars acclaim Marshack's work as a dramatic breakthrough in the study of early man; others still question his interpretations.

To anyone today scanning the long panorama of Cro-Magnon times, as it stretches from some 40,000 years ago towards the beginnings of agriculture, metalworking and cities, by far the greater portion of it is shrouded in mist and blurred by deceiving shadows. Yet as the more random shreds of evidence are carefully pieced together by archaeologists and anthropologists around the world, the closer seem the people who lived then. Inwardly, modern man knows that he still shares many of the same fears and aspirations as his ancient brethren of the Stone Age, and needs the same kind of assurances. As archaeologist Grahame Clark of Cambridge University observes, "Prehistory is not something human beings lived through long ago. It is with us still."

After the Ice Age, a Lusty Society of Bowmen-Artists

Towards the close of the age of the great hunter-gatherers, not long before the agricultural way of life took hold in Europe, men and women still inhabited caves and rock shelters, and they continued to paint on the walls. But, as rock paintings from some 100 open-air sites in eastern Spain show, artists there were putting a new and revealing emphasis on man. Whereas the earlier cave art of Altamira and Lascaux typically portrays large, naturalistic animals, the later, so-called Spanish Levantine paintings are stylized, often anecdotal works that for the first time in the history of art depict men, women and children in social groups.

These lively scenes reveal much about life 4,500 to 11,500 years ago. Hunting remained as important an activity as it had been earlier, but hunters, like the one at left, now felled their prey—and sometimes each other —with bow and arrow, a relatively recent invention. But as some of the later paintings hint, these people may also have had a few domesticated cattle to fall back on when the hunters returned empty-handed.

The paintings themselves might be interpreted as a surer sign of important progress. The mere fact that man replaced animals as the dominant subject of art suggests that, some 30,000 years after he had evolved into his modern form, he faced his world with a new sense of self-confidence.

A hunter draws his double-curved bow, an advanced weapon that increased his range.

A Zest for Hunting with Bow and Arrow

Hunting dominates the art of the Spanish Levantine people and, as the scene at left suggests, they pursued the activity with zest—perhaps as a result of the pride they took in their skill with bow and arrow. The recently invented weapon gave the hunters an advantage over their spear-wielding ancestors. Not only were bows and arrows lighter than the stout-shafted spears and thus easier to carry, but they called for less muscle power to shoot, had a greater range and, better yet, they were—in the hands of a skilled archer—a great deal more accurate. It has been estimated that a hunter using a bow like the one depicted at left could shoot an arrow that had enough force to kill an ibex at a range of 30 to 40 yards. And if he missed his target, he usually had the chance to shoot another arrow right away.

Two bowmen shoot at a jumping ibex as a third archer approaches.

A hunter flees for his life in a scene that also includes the animal chasing him (above right), a wounded and enraged wild bull. This and the scene at top may have been painted as reminders of specific historical events, though some experts interpret them as ritual offerings to ensure bountiful hunts in the future, believing that the paintings mark places of worship.

A hunter aims the fatal arrow at a stag, which has apparently been exhausted and brought to bay by a long chase. The small animal behind the stag is probably a domesticated dog—perhaps the first one to be represented in art.

A New Capacity for Strife

Though fighting is rarely considered a sign of progress, disciplined combat signalled advances in social organization. Several scenes in Spanish Levantine art show bands of archers attacking each other, although it seems the fights were more in the nature of displays of energy and courage than seriously purposeful warfare. In a few paintings, larger-than-average figures in elaborate trappings (*below*) suggest a simple form of military ranking; the death of such leaders in battle is portrayed with special feeling and detail. Evidence of even greater social sophistication can be seen in the dramatic painting known as *The Execution* (*far right*). The offence of the victim is uncertain; he may be a criminal or an enemy. But the obvious formality of his death indicates the existence of a code regulating behaviour.

Five archers advance single file with their weapons at the ready. The man in front appears to be the leader, set apart by his tall, elaborate headdress.

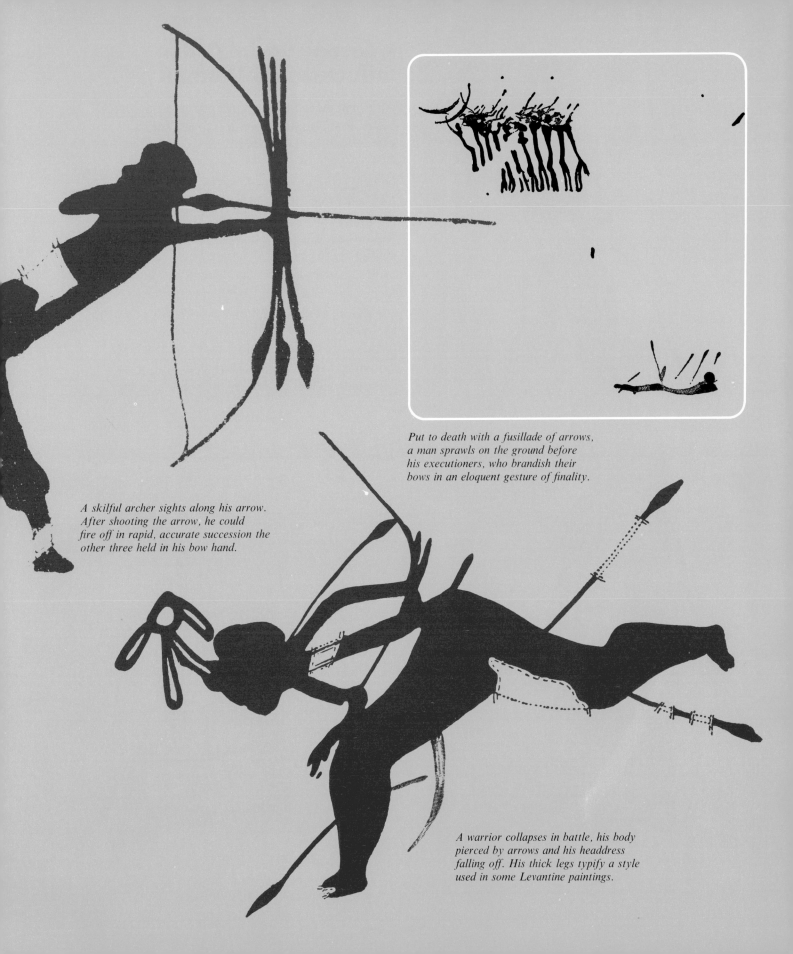

A skilful archer sights along his arrow. After shooting the arrow, he could fire off in rapid, accurate succession the other three held in his bow hand.

Put to death with a fusillade of arrows, a man sprawls on the ground before his executioners, who brandish their bows in an eloquent gesture of finality.

A warrior collapses in battle, his body pierced by arrows and his headdress falling off. His thick legs typify a style used in some Levantine paintings.

A Lasting Social Order Influenced by Women

Although the paintings depict no settlement or permanent dwelling, several intimate scenes convey a sense of community and of patterned social life. The women presumably did homely chores, gathered nuts and berries, and chatted together while the men were off hunting. If the painting at far right of a mother holding a child's hand is any indication, they brought up their children with genuine affection. The women also took part in feasts and religious ceremonies (*below*) that could bring together two or more wandering groups sharing the same culture. When these seminomads eventually settled down to farming, the social traditions they had developed as hunters formed a framework that doubtless persisted and lent stability to the new way of life.

Bare-breasted, a woman wears a loincloth of leather.

A woman strolls with her child, whose hair is pulled up in twin puffs. Such paintings of a single child suggest that the hunters' families were small—and probably not just because of a high infant-mortality rate. In recent times among some hunter-gatherers, women with too many children are known to have practised infanticide and crude forms of birth control and abortion.

Circling in pairs around a male figure, women perform what appears to be a ceremonial dance. The animals surrounding them are mostly wild; but the two striped bovine beasts seen at far left might well have been very early specimens of domesticated cattle.

The Emergence of Man

This chart records the progression of life on earth from its first appearance in the warm waters of the new-formed planet through the evolution of man himself; it traces his physical, social, technological and intellectual development to the Christian era. To place these advances in commonly used chronological sequences, the column at the

Geology	Archaeology	Thousand Millions of Years Ago	
Precambrian earliest era		4.5	Creation of the Earth
		4	Formation of the primordial sea
		3	First life, single-celled algae and bacteria, appears in water
		2	
		1	

		Millions of Years Ago	
			First oxygen-breathing animals appear
		800	
			Primitive organisms develop interdependent specialized cells
		600	Shell-bearing multicelled invertebrate animals appear
Palaeozoic ancient life			Evolution of armoured fish, first animals to possess backbones
		400	Small amphibians venture on to land
			Reptiles and insects arise
			Thecodont, ancestor of dinosaurs, arises
Mesozoic middle life		200	Age of dinosaurs begins
			Birds appear
			Mammals live in shadow of dinosaurs
			Age of dinosaurs ends
		80	
			Prosimians, earliest primates, develop in trees
Cainozoic recent life		60	
		40	Monkeys and apes evolve
		20	
		10	Ramapithecus, oldest known primate with apparently man-like traits, evolves in India and Africa
		8	
		6	Australopithecus, closest primate ancestor to man, appears in Africa
		4	

Geology	Archaeology	Millions of Years Ago	
Lower Pleistocene oldest period of most recent epoch	**Lower Palaeolithic** oldest period of Old Stone Age	2	Oldest known tool fashioned by man in Africa
			First true man, Homo erectus, emerges in East Indies and Africa
		1	Homo erectus populates temperate zones

		Thousands of Years Ago	
Middle Pleistocene middle period of most recent epoch		800	Man learns to control and use fire
		600	
			Large-scale, organized elephant hunts staged in Europe
		400	Man begins to make artificial shelters from branches
		200	
Upper Pleistocene latest period of most recent epoch	**Middle Palaeolithic** middle period of Old Stone Age		Neanderthal man emerges in Europe
		80	
		60	Ritual burials in Europe and Middle East suggest belief in afterlife
			Woolly mammoths hunted by Neanderthal in northern Europe
		40	Cave bear becomes focus of cult in Europe
	Upper Palaeolithic latest period of Old Stone Age		**Cro-Magnon man arises in Europe**
			Asian hunters cross Bering Land Bridge to populate New World
			Oldest known written record, lunar notations on bone, made in Europe
			Man reaches Australia
			First artists decorate walls and ceilings of caves in France and Spain
		30	**Figurines sculpted for nature worship**
		20	**Invention of needle makes sewing possible**
			Bison hunting begins on Great Plains of North America
Holocene present epoch	**Mesolithic** Middle Stone Age	10	**Bow and arrow invented in Europe**
			Pottery first made in Japan

(vertical label: Last Ice Age)

▼ Four thousand million years ago ▼ Three thousand million years ago

▲ Origin of the Earth (4,500 million) ▲ First life (3,500 million)

left of each of the chart's four sections identifies the great geological eras into which the earth's history is divided by scientists, while the second column lists the archaeological ages of human history. The key dates in the rise of life and of man's outstanding accomplishments appear in the third column (years and events mentioned in this volume of The Emergence of Man appear in bold type). The chart is not to scale; the reason is made clear by the bar below, which represents in linear scale the 4,500 million years spanned by the chart—on the scaled bar, the portion relating to the total period of known human existence (*far right*) is too small to be distinguished.

Geology	Archaeology	Years B.C.	
Holocene (cont.)	Neolithic New Stone Age	9000	
			Sheep domesticated in Middle East
			Dog domesticated in North America
		8000	Jericho, oldest known city, settled
			Goat domesticated in Persia
			Man cultivates his first crops, wheat and barley, in Middle East
		7000	Pattern of village life grows in Middle East
			Catal Hüyük, in what is now Turkey, becomes largest Neolithic city
			Loom invented in Middle East
			Cattle domesticated in Middle East
		6000	Agriculture begins to replace hunting in Europe
			Copper used in trade in Mediterranean area
	Copper Age		Corn cultivated in Mexico
		4800	Oldest known massive stone monument built in Brittany
		4000	Sail-propelled boats used in Egypt
			First city-states develop in Sumer
			Cylinder seals begin to be used as marks of identification in Middle East
		3500	First potatoes grown in South America
			Wheel originates in Sumer
			Man begins to cultivate rice in Far East
			Silk moth domesticated in China
			Horse domesticated in south Russia
			Egyptian merchant trading ships start to ply the Mediterranean
			Pictograph writing invented in Middle East
		3000	Bronze first used to make tools in Middle East
	Bronze Age		City life spreads to Nile Valley
			Plough is developed in Middle East
			Accurate calendar based on stellar observation devised in Egypt
		2800	Stonehenge, most famous of ancient stone monuments, begun in England
			Pyramids built in Egypt
		2600	Variety of gods and heroes glorified in *Gilgamesh* and other epics in Middle East

Geology	Archaeology	Years B.C.	
Holocene (cont.)	Bronze Age (cont.)	2500	Cities rise in the Indus Valley
			Earliest evidence of use of skis in Scandinavia
			Earliest written code of laws drawn up in Sumer
		2000	
			Use of bronze in Europe
			Chicken and elephant domesticated in Indus Valley
			Eskimo culture begins in Bering Strait area
		1500	Invention of ocean-going outrigger canoes enables man to reach islands of South Pacific
			Ceremonial bronze sculptures created in China
			Imperial government, ruling distant provinces, established by Hittites
		1400	Iron in use in Middle East
			First complete alphabet devised in script of the Ugarit people in Syria
			Hebrews introduce concept of monotheism
	Iron Age	1000	Reindeer domesticated in Eurasia
			Phoenicians spread alphabet
		900	
		800	Use of iron begins to spread throughout Europe
			First highway system built in Assyria
			Homer composes *Iliad* and *Odyssey*
			Mounted nomads appear in the Middle East as a new and powerful force
		700	Rome founded
			Wheel barrow invented in China
		200	Epics about India's gods and heroes, the *Mahabharata* and *Ramayana*, written
			Water wheel invented in Middle East
		0	Christian era begins

▼ Two thousand million years ago   ▼ One thousand million years ago

First oxygen-breathing animals (900 million) ▲   First animals to possess ▲ backbones (470 million)   First men (2 million) ▲

Credits

The sources for the illustrations in this book are shown below. Credits from left to right are separated by semicolons, from top to bottom by dashes.

All photographs by Jean Vertut appearing in this book are reproduced through the courtesy of Editions Mazenod, Paris.
Cover—Painting by Burt Silverman, background photograph by Ralph Morse for LIFE. 8—Dr. Léon Pales, Musée de l'Homme. 12,13 —Novosti Press Agency, except top right, drawing by Walter Johnson after Mikhail Gerasimov. 17—Drawings by Nicholas Fasciano. 20—Enrico Ferorelli. 21—Map by Lothar Roth. 22,23—Enrico Ferorelli. 27 to 33 —Paintings by Burt Silverman. 34—Novosti Press Agency. 38,39—Map by Lothar Roth. 41—Robert Edwards, South Australian Museum. 42—Novosti Press Agency. 46—Ken Kay courtesy Dr. N. J. Shackleton, University of Cambridge. 47—Jacques Evenou courtesy Jean Bouchud, National Center for Scientific Research, Paris. 49—Jerry Pace courtesy Dr. Philip E. Smith, University of Montreal. 51 to 59—Paintings by Chet Jezierski. 60—Pierre Boulat courtesy Musée des Antiquités Nationales Saint-Germain-en-Laye. 64—Jean Vertut, Musée de Les Eyzies. 67—Pierre Laurent, extrait de *Heureuse Préhistoire*. 68,69—Charts by Earl L. Kvam. 72 to 75—Drawings by Arno Sternglass. 76—Patrimoine de l'Institut Royal des Sciences Naturelles de Belgique. 79—Masachika Suhara courtesy Professor Chosuke Serizawa. 80—Bedrich Kocek courtesy Brno Antropos Museum. 83—Pierre Boulat courtesy J. Tixier. 84 to 91—Pierre Boulat courtesy J. Tixier, except pictures appearing far right on pages 85, 87, 89 and 91, Richard Jeffery courtesy J. Tixier. 92—Photo Musée d'Aquitaine, cliché Vertut. 96—Jean Vertut, Collection Saint-Périer, except far right, Bedrich Kocek courtesy Brno Antropos Museum. 98 —Bedrich Kocek courtesy Brno Antropos Museum; Collection Musée de l'Homme. 99 —Collection Musée de l'Homme; Musei Civici, Reggio Emilia; Novosti Press Agency. 100—Novosti Press Agency; Jean Vertut, Musée de l'Homme. 102—Reportage photographique YAN courtesy Musée des Antiquités Nationales Saint-Germain-en-Laye. 104,105—Jean Vertut, Musée des Antiquités Nationales Saint-Germain-en-Laye—Jean Vertut, Musée de Périgueux; From *L'Art Pendant l'Age du Renne* by E. Piette, Paris, 1907, Musée des Antiquités Nationales Saint-Germain-en-Laye courtesy Paolo Graziosi; Jean Vertut, Musée des Antiquités Nationales Saint-Germain-en-Laye. 107—Collection Musée de l'Homme. 109—Cliché Conservation des Monuments Historiques de Périgueux, Reproduction Interdite. 110—Jean Vertut—Photo René Vital. 111—Docteur Jacques Bauer, Institut de Photographie Scientifique et Médicale, Faculté de Marseille, except left, Photo René Vital. 112, 113—Courtesy French Government Tourist Office. 115—Alain Roussot. 116, 117—Jean Vertut, except bottom left, from: *Préhistoire de l'Art Occidental*, André Leroi-Gourhan, Editions Mazenod, Paris, photo Jean Vertut. 118 to 121—Jean Vertut. 122, 123 —From *Préhistoire de l'Art Occidental*, André Leroi-Gourhan, Editions Mazenod, Paris, photo Jean Vertut. 124,125—Jean Vertut, except top right, Pierre Belzeaux-Rapho, courtesy Louis Plassard. 126—Drawing by the late Henri Breuil, courtesy of Breuil's executor Arnold Fawcus. 129—Photo Collection Bégouën, cliché Jean Vertut. 130—Copyright Colorphoto Hans Hinz, Basel. 132 —Photothèque André Held-ZIOLO; Morton H. Levine. 133—Photo Romain Robert. 134 —Jean Vertut. 135—Photo Romain Robert; Photothèque André Held-ZIOLO. 136— Courtesy of The American Museum of Natural History. 139—Novosti Press Agency. 140,141—Copyright © Alexander Marshack 1973, after Alexander Marshack, *The Roots of Civilization*, McGraw-Hill Book Company, 1972. 143—Pierre Boulat, courtesy J. Tixier—Drawing by Nicholas Fasciano. 145 to 151—From *Art in the Ice Age: Spanish, Levant Art, Arctic Art* by Johannes Maringer and Hans-Georg Bandi, Praeger Publishers, New York, 1953.

Acknowledgments

For the help given in the preparation of this book, the editors are indebted to Maurice Baudet, Grotte de Cougnac, France; Jacques Bauer, Medical Faculty, Institute of Scientific and Medical Photography, Marseilles, France; Megan Biesele, Austin, Texas; François Bordes, Professor of Geology, University of Bordeaux, France; Jean Bouchud, Research Supervisor, National Centre for Scientific Research, Paris; Michel Brézillon, Director of Prehistoric Antiquities for the Region of Paris; Bernard Campbell, Professor of Anthropology, University of California, Los Angeles; Piero Cassoli, Director, Italian Institute of Human Palaeontology, Rome; Glen Cole, Department of Anthropology, The Field Museum of Natural History, Chicago; Gérard Cordier, Research Assistant, National Centre for Scientific Research, Paris; David Damas, Department of Anthropology, McMaster University, Hamilton, Ontario; Michael Dauvois, Head Designer, National Centre for Scientific Research, Paris; Henri Delporte, Curator of the National Museums, Museum of National Antiquities, Saint-Germain-en-Laye, France; Jean Gaussen, Meuvic-sur-l'Isle, Dordogne, France; Paolo Graziosi, Director, Institute of Palaeontology, Florence University, Florence, Italy; Raymond Grosset, Rapho-Paris; Jean Guichard, Curator of the National Museum of Prehistory, Les Eyzies, France; Bruce Heezen, Associate Professor of Geology, Department of Geology, Columbia University, New York City; Jean de Heinzelin, Scientific Consultant, The Royal Belgian Institute of Natural Sciences, Brussels; David M. Hopkins, Research Geologist, Office of Marine Geology, U.S. Geological Survey, Menlo Park, California; Sidney S. Horenstein, Scientific Assistant, The American Museum of Natural History, New York City; Marie-Louise Inizan, Paris; Daniel Julien, Assistant Manager, Zoological Garden of St. Félicien, Lac St.-Jean, Quebec; Georges Lagorse, Les Eyzies, France; Pierre Laurent, Bordeaux, France; Jacques Leclerc, Paris; Richard B. Lee, Department of Anthropology, University of Toronto, Toronto, Ontario; Marcel Lefèvre, Director of the Laboratory, National Centre for Scientific Research, Paris; Jean-Pierre Lehman, Professor at the Institute of Palaeontology, Museum of Natural History, Paris; André Leroi-Gourhan, Professor of Prehistory, Collège de France, Paris; Arlette Leroi-Gourhan, Director, Talynology Laboratory, Museum of Man, Paris; Morton Levine, Professor of Anthropology, Fordham

University, New York City; Alexander Marshack, Research Associate, Peabody Museum of Archaeology and Ethnology, Harvard University, Cambridge, Massachusetts; Lucien Mazenod, Paris; Léon Pales, Director of Research, National Centre for Scientific Research, Paris; Louis Plassard, Grotte de Rouffignac, France; Romain Robert, Tarascon-sur-Ariège, France; Alain Roussot, Bordeaux; Max Sarradet, Curator of Lascaux Cave, Lascaux, France; N. J. Shackleton, of the Sub-Department of Quaternary Research, University of Cambridge, England; Denise de Sonneville-Bordes, Research Supervisor, National Centre for Scientific Research, Paris; Michel Soubeyran, Curator of the Périgord Museum, Périgueux, France; John B. Speth, Assistant Professor of Anthropology, Hunter College, New York City; Jacques Tixier, Research Supervisor, National Centre for Scientific Research, Paris; Jan Van Donk, Research Associate, Lamont-Doherty Geological Observatory, Palisades, New York; Jean Vertut, Paris.

Bibliography

Bandi, Breuil, Holm, Lhote, Lommel, *The Art of the Stone Age.* Crown Publishers, Inc., 1961.

Berndt, Ronald M. and Catherine H., *The World of the First Australians.* The University of Chicago Press, 1964.

Bibby, Geoffrey, *The Testimony of the Spade.* Alfred A. Knopf, 1956.

Birket-Smith, Kaj, *Eskimos.* Crown Publishers, Inc., 1971.

Bishop, Walter W., and J. Desmond Clark, eds., *Background to Evolution in Africa.* University of Chicago Press, 1968.

Bordaz, Jacques, *Tools of the Old and New Stone Age,* David and Charles, 1971.

Bordes, François:
A Tale of Two Caves. Harper & Row, 1972.
Old Stone Age. Weidenfeld and Nicolson, 1968.

Brace, C. Loring, *Stages of Human Evolution,* Prentice-Hall, 1967.

Braidwood, R. J. and Willey, G. R., eds., *Courses Toward Urban Life,* Edinburgh University Press.

Bray, Warwick, and David Trump, *Dictionary of Archaeology,* A. Lane, 1970, Penguin Books, 1972.

Breuil, Abbé H., *Four Hundred Centuries of Cave Art.* Centre d'Études et de Documentation Préhistoriques.

Broderick, Alan Houghton, *Father of Prehistory.* William Morrow & Company, 1963.

Butzer, Karl W., *Environment and Archaeology,* Methuen, 1972.

Campbell, Bernard Grant, *Human Evolution,* Heinemann Educational Books, 1967.

Campbell, Joseph, *The Masks of God: Primitive Mythology.* The Viking Press, 1959.

Cheng Te-K'un, *New Light on Prehistoric China,* Heffer, 1966.

Clark, Grahame, *Aspects of Prehistory.* University of California Press, 1970.

Clark, J. Desmond, *The Prehistory of Africa.* Praeger Publishers, 1970.

Clark, J. G. D., *Prehistoric Europe, the Economic Basis.* Philosophical Library, 1952.

Cole, Sonia, *The Prehistory of East Africa.* The New American Library, 1965.

Coon, Carleton S.:
The Hunting Peoples. Little, Brown and Company, 1971.
Origin of Races, Cape, 1963.
The Story of Man. Alfred A. Knopf, 1970.

Daniel, Glyn A.:
A Hundred Years of Archaeology. Gerald Duckworth and Co., Ltd., 1950.
Hungry Archaeologist in France, Faber, 1963.
Idea of Prehistory, Penguin Books, 1964.
Origins and Growth of Archaeology, Penguin Books, 1967.

Denes, Peter B., and Elliot N. Pinson, *The Speech Chain: The Physics and Biology of Spoken Language.* Anchor Books, 1973.

Dobzhansky, Theodosius:
Genetics and the Origin of the Species, Columbia University Press, 1971.
Heredity and the Nature of Man, Allen and Unwin, 1965.

Dolhinow, Phyllis, and Vincent M. Sarich, eds., *Background for Man: Readings in Physical Anthropology.* Little, Brown and Company, 1971.

Dunbar, Carl Owen and Waage, Karl M., *Historical Geology,* John Wiley, 1970.

Fairservis, Walter A., Jr., *The Roots of Ancient India.* The Macmillan Company, 1971.

Flint, Richard Foster, *Glacial and Quaternary Geology,* John Wiley, 1971.

Garn, Stanley M.:
Human Races. Charles C. Thomas, 1961.
ed., *Readings on Race.* Charles C. Thomas, 1960.

Gernet, Jacques, *Ancient China,* Faber, 1968.

Giedion, Siegfried, *The Eternal Present,* Oxford University Press, 1962. (Vol. 1), 1964. (Vol. 2).

Graziosi, Paolo, *Palaeolithic Art,* Faber, 1960.

Hooton, Earnest Albert, *Up from the Ape.* The Macmillan Company, 1946.

Howells, William, *Mankind in the Making.* Doubleday & Company, Inc., 1967.

Hulse, Frederick S., *The Human Species: An Introduction to Physical Anthropology.* Random House, 1971.

Klein, Richard G., *Man and Culture in the Late Pleistocene.* Chandler Publishing Company, 1969.

Kranzberg, Melvin, and Carroll W. Pursell, Jr., eds., *Technology in Western Civilization,* Vol. 1. Oxford University Press, 1967.

Kurtén, Björn:
The Ice Age. G. P. Putnam's Sons, 1972.
Pleistocene Mammals of Europe. Weidenfeld and Nicolson, 1968.

Laming, Annette, *Lascaux.* Penguin Books Ltd., 1959.

Leakey, Louis S. B., *Adam's Ancestors: The Evolution of Man and His Culture.* Harper & Brothers, 1960.

Leroi-Gourhan, André, *Treasures of Prehistoric Art.* Harry N. Abrams, Inc.

Lommel, Andreas, *Shamanism.* McGraw-Hill Book Company, 1967.

McBurney, C. B. M., *The Stone Age in Northern Africa.* Penguin Books, 1960.

Maringer, Johannes, *The Gods of Prehistoric Man.* Weidenfeld and Nicolson, 1960.

Maringer, Johannes, and Hans-Georg Bandi, in execution of a plan by Hugo Obermaier, *Art in the Ice Age.* Frederick A. Praeger, 1953.

Marshack, Alexander, *The Roots of Civilization.* McGraw-Hill Book Company, 1972.

Michael, Henry N., ed., *Studies in Siberian Shamanism.* University of Toronto Press, 1963.

Mulvaney, D. J. and J. Gordon, *Aboriginal Man and Environment in Australia.* Aus-

tralian National University Press, 1971.
Oakley, Kenneth P.:
Framework for Dating Fossil Man. Weidenfeld and Nicholson, 1969.
Man the Tool-maker. British Museum, 1963.
Pfeiffer, John E.:
Emergence of Man. Nelson, 1970.
Search for Early Man. Caravel Books, Cassell, 1969.
Semenov, S. A., *Prehistoric Technology.*

Adams and Dart, 1970.
Simpson, George Gaylord:
The Geography of Evolution. Capricorn Books, 1967.
The Major Features of Evolution. Simon and Schuster, 1953.
Stern, Philip Van Doren, *Prehistoric Europe.* Allen and Unwin, 1970.
Triestman, Judith M., *The Prehistory of China: An Archaeological Exploration.* Double-

day & Company, Inc., 1972.
Turnbull, Colin M., *The Forest People.* Simon and Schuster, 1962.
Ucko, Peter J., and Andrée Rosenfeld, *Palaeolithic Cave Art.* Weidenfeld and Nicolson, 1967.
Washburn, Sherwood L., *Social Life of Early Man.* Aldine Publishing Company, 1961.
Wendt, Herbert, *In Search of Adam.* Houghton Mifflin Company, 1956.

Index

Numerals in italics indicate an illustration of the subject mentioned.

XXXX

Filmsetting by C. E. Dawkins (Typesetters) Ltd., London, SE1 1UN
Printed and bound in Belgium by Brepols Fabrieken N.V.